Corporate Actions –
A Concise Guide

An introduction to securities events

by Francis Groves

HARRIMAN HOUSE LTD

3A Penns Road
Petersfield
Hampshire
GU32 2EW
GREAT BRITAIN

Tel: +44 (0)1730 233870
Fax: +44 (0)1730 233880
Email: enquiries@harriman-house.com
Website: www.harriman-house.com
First published as hardback in Great Britain in 2008, this paperback edition published in 2012.

978-0-85719-217-2

British Library Cataloguing in Publication Data
A CIP catalogue record for this book can be obtained from the British Library.

Printed and bound in Great Britain by the CPI Group, Antony Rowe.

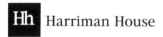 Harriman House

Contents

1. Defining Corporate Actions   **1**

The characteristics of a share and its issuer – definitions of corporate actions – how the action is decided upon: articles of association, AGMs & EGMs – the board of directors – chief financial officers and treasury departments – legislation underpinning the system.

2. The Main Corporate Actions   **9**

How many types of corporate action are there? – definitions/descriptions of main types of corporate actions (dividends, scrip dividends, scrip issues, return of capital, consolidation, rights issues, takeover bids, agreed takeovers, de-mergers) – benefits or otherwise for shareholders and share prices.

3. The Corporate Actions Process   **31**

From the investor's point of view – announcement dates – record dates – ex-dates – effective dates – steps along the way to a takeover – corporate actions information from the share prices pages – typical timetables for returns of capital and rights issues.

12. Corporate Action Effects Across the Investing Spectrum 147

How corporate actions affect the calculation of stock exchange indices – how charts handle corporate actions – the effects of corporate actions on futures, options, CFDs and ETFs – corporate actions for CDOs – corporate actions and securities lending – hedge funds and corporate actions – corporate actions and the pension fund trustee – corporate actions and crime.

About the Author

Francis Groves studied modern history at the London School of Economics and has many years of experience working for legal and financial publishers including, Reuters, the Financial Times and Butterworths. He has written on overseas property investment and created financial literacy training materials. The interaction of politics and finance is a particular interest for him.

Francis is also the author of *Exchange Traded Funds: A Concise Guide to ETFs* (Harriman House, 2011).

Preface

What the book covers

Corporate actions are normally considered as incidental to the business of investing and marketing investments, but the aim of this concise guide is to look at the subject of corporate actions in the round, defining what corporate actions are, listing and describing the main corporate actions and showing how individual corporate actions are applied to investors' holdings of securities. This will give an overview of the way in which the corporate actions processing function works both in the UK and other important global markets. Detailing all the differences between jurisdictions is beyond the scope of this guide, though the UK is taken as a starting point to help describe and explain significant national distinctions, particularly for the United States and the rest of the European Union.

Who the book is for

The guide is designed to be an introduction to corporate actions for investment industry practitioners in general. Those starting out in corporate actions processing will find it a helpful outline, but it is also designed to be useful for all who encounter corporate actions tangentially in disciplines such as fund management or financial advice provision. Different industry participants have differing interests in corporate actions, and for the sake of consistency the guide is (mainly) written from the point of view of the beneficial owners of securities.

How the book is structured

Those who simply require a handy and straightforward introduction to specific corporate actions will find the quick guide to the content and the glossary of corporate actions terms especially useful.

The first three chapters deal exclusively with equity corporate actions. These chapters cover definitions of a corporate action and the legal framework(s) underpinning corporate actions, followed by a look at the most significant actions one by one, and then a detailed examination of the staging of some of these. The corporate actions of debt securities are given separate treatment in Chapter 11.

In Chapters 4, 5 and 6 the focus moves from the corporate actions themselves to the industry that has grown up to process them. These three chapters cover respectively the corporate actions industry, its efficiency and its progress (recent and future).

Chapter 7 looks at the impact of successive corporate actions on one particular share (Encore Oil) and shareholdings in it. This is followed by a look at the scope investors have for influencing such events through shareholder voting.

The final chapter looks at how corporate actions are treated in the context of stock indices, stock charts and a number of more complex investments.

Although change in the corporate actions industry is sometimes slow (it has been described as glacial) the process is always evolving, and so this guide can only aim to be a snapshot of the state of affairs at the time of writing, together with an outline of some of the forces for change that are at work. The aim has been to provide sufficient detail to give the reader a working model that is practically helpful in navigating the corporate actions universe.

Introduction

Corporate actions have been sidelined for too long and deserve to be treated with more respect. No type of investment security can be fully understood without knowledge of its corporate actions. All corporate actions have implications for the sustainability of an investment's performance, but more beguiling investment preoccupations put them into the shade.

The corporate actions processing industry is in deeper shadow than even the actions themselves. Together with bank clearing and exchange settlement systems, the administration of corporate actions is one of the key co-operative functions tying our highly competitive global finance industry together. In the financial markets of the developed world the efficiency and "risklessness" of corporate actions processing is entirely taken for granted. Yet the volume of complex corporate actions and a common sense estimate of the likelihood of mistakes occurring suggest that industry practitioners and investing clients may be deluding themselves.

Figures for the annual number of equity and debt security corporate actions stand at approximately one million and three million respectively.[1] For equities it is estimated that corporate actions that can be classed as complex comprise 10-15% of the total. It has also been estimated that every year 18,000 corporate actions have the potential to cause significant share price movements in the world's 25 most

---

[1] For the 12 months from March 2003 there were estimated to be 935,000 equity corporate actions ('Corporate Action Processing, What Are The Risks', a study carried out by the consultancy Oxera on behalf of the Depository Trust and Clearing Corporation). Figures on the volume of complex actions and those with the potential to cause share price movements are from the same report.

important stock markets. Although this represents just a small percentage of the total number of corporate actions, it nevertheless equates to several dozen price moving corporate events each trading day. In the realm of debt securities the payment events of structured debt caused a huge increase in the volume and complexity of corporate actions in the 2003-07 period.[2] Corporate actions processing faces challenges in delivering entitlements to investors accurately and in good time and meeting these challenges is important to the securities industry. Despite this corporate action practitioners have been left to themselves, carrying on their craft quietly behind a high wall.

If knowledge of corporate actions brings us to fully understand the securities they relate to, some familiarity with corporate actions processing is important in gaining an insight into the workings of the securities industry as a system. With the exceptions of accountancy and financial regulation, no other activity involves as many kinds of investment industry participant as corporate actions processing.

The current state of corporate actions underscores the incompleteness of the globalisation of financial markets. The corporate actions industry is global in the sense that the corporate actions for any tradable security, from wherever it originates will, in some cases, only be processed after a fashion. The relegation of corporate action processing to obscurity is one factor in disguising the host of cultural, ethical and regulatory differences that distinguish securities markets from one another. These differences in the detail are woven into much cross-border corporate actions processing. Although we may be on the brink of an unparalleled extension of the world's developed economies, understanding of the entitlements of shareholders (domestic and overseas) in the newly developed countries is a long way behind other features of globalisation.

---

[2] 'Transforming Structured Securities Processing' (Depository Trust & Clearing Corporation white paper, September 2007).

A look at corporate actions at this time will give food for thought in several directions. As the financial institutions take stock, re-examining their points of reference, it will be interesting to see whether corporate action entitlements receive more of the limelight than they have up until now.

The corporate actions industry needs to improve its efficiency; what needs to change to affect this, and will the major players be able or willing to put up the investment necessary? As the balance of economic power shifts eastwards, what kind of corporate actions environment will investors meet with when they invest outside their own region? In sum, a better acquaintance with the current state of corporate actions will allow a greater understanding of changes in the securities industry.

Quick Guide to Locating Information on Specific Corporate Actions

Corporate Action	Where to look	Related Topics
Bonus Issue (Scrip Issue, Capitalisation Issue, Stock split)	Chs.2,3	Share Consolidation Ch.2
Consolidation	Chs. 2,7	
Conversion	Ch.11	
Dividends	Chs.2,3,10	Dividend Yield Ch.2 Dividend Cover Ch.2 Scrip Dividend Ch.2
Interest Payments	Ch.11	Accrued Interest Ch.11
Redemption	Ch.11	Partial Redemption Ch.11 Drawing Ch.11
Return of Capital (Capital Distribution)	Chs.2,3	Capital Gains Tax Ch.9
Rights Issue (Share Placing)	Chs.2,3	Other types of share placing Ch.7, Appendix IIII Dilution Ch.7 Capital Gains Tax Ch.9 Pre-emption Rights Ch.2, Appendix III
Scrip Dividends	Ch.2	
Share Buyback	Ch.2	
Takeover Bid	Chs.2,3,5,8,	Agreed Takeover Ch.2 De-merger/Divestment /Spin off Chs.2,8,9 Reverse Takeover Chs.7,8 Capital Gains Tax Ch.9
Voting	Chs.8,10	
Warrant	Ch.11	

1.

Defining Corporate Actions

Investors may focus mainly on the purchase of securities and their re-sale but equities and debt securities are more than passive tokens of investment value. By means of corporate actions they acquire a life of their own, an ability to transform themselves and to make investors change their minds. Individual corporate actions for equities such as takeover bids or rights issues can have a significant effect on share prices. Over just a few years, the cumulative effect of a number of corporate actions can cause a share to undergo a complete metamorphosis.

The starting point of all corporate actions is the ownership of individual units of investment; shares, bonds or variations. For shares of **common stock**, the type of security on which we shall be concentrating chiefly, the overarching right is that of ownership of the company in question (the issuer) and from ownership spring the following specific rights:

1. To elect the board of directors

2. To vote for corporate actions that require shareholder approval

3. To share in corporate earnings in the form of dividends

4. To maintain the same proportion of the company's common stock in the event of additional shares being issued

And, finally,

5. To receive a share of the **residual assets** of the company in the event of liquidation (which could be called the saddest corporate action of them all)

So, along with ownership come shared control, shared benefits and rules to protect the rights attached to each share. The shared control tends not to translate into power for the small investor or even large minority shareholdings and rules protecting the rights attached to each of a company's shares do not necessarily protect the financial interests of the share's owner.[3]

Further definitions

Definitions of "corporate action" vary depending upon whether the point of view is that of the issuer:

'an event initiated by a company that affects its share,' (Frances Maguire, The Banker, 1st June 2007)

'A corporate action occurs when changes are made to the capital structure or financial position of an issuer of a security that affect any of the securities it has issued.' ('Transforming Corporate Action Processing', Depository Trust & Clearing Corporation, 2003)

or the shareholder:

> ...where the owner of a security is given the opportunity to receive a benefit or participate in a reorganisation of the company.

A complete definition covering all types of corporate action may not be possible. The important point is that corporate actions all have their genesis in the entitlements that accompany owning the shares (no matter how few of them). It follows from this that, in order to put corporate actions into effect, comprehensive information about the ownership of all the shares concerned is required. This information is held in the company's **share register**.

---

[3] The shareholder's lack of control over events affecting their investment will be looked at in more detail in Chapter 7.

How are corporate actions decided?

For each company the workings of corporate actions will be set out in the articles of association. If one thought of a company as a country, the memorandum and articles of association would be the country's constitution, the shares would be the voters and the place of Congress or Parliament would be taken by the shareholder meetings (annual or extraordinary general meetings). Although this looks like a "winner takes all" system of government, some proposals, known as "special resolutions", require 75% support.[4] Proposals to change the memorandum and articles of association would be treated as special resolutions.

Chapter 8 will take another look at voting in shareholder meetings; how it works, how effective it is and moves afoot to improve the system.

Decisions on corporate actions or changes to the articles of association are not the only purpose of shareholder meetings; they also (for example) vote to approve the remuneration of directors, to elect directors, or re-elect them when their terms of office expire.

In the analogy of a country the directors are, of course, the government. In almost all circumstances it is they who make proposals on various corporate actions for the shareholder meetings to decide on.

Generally speaking, ensuring that a company has sufficient capital and cash to carry on its business successfully will be the responsibility of the company's Chief Financial Officer (CFO) and its treasury department. Recommendations about items such as the dividend, share or bond issues and share buybacks will originate from this quarter.

---

[4] The significance of the 75% hurdle for special resolutions was demonstrated at the Northern Rock EGM in January 2008 when a number of rebel resolutions received the support of the simple majorities of shareholders represented, but failed because support fell short of the 75% level. As a rule, reporting on shareholder meetings in the press is strong on comment and short on detail. The most detailed source of information is likely to be the website of the company in question.

Patterns of organisation and chains of command vary from one company to the next, but a company's annual report should explain how the treasury function is carried out.

Who writes the rules?

The picture of the sovereignty of shareholder meetings over the affairs of the company distorts reality by ignoring the importance of national (and international) legislation in regulating companies' affairs. In the United Kingdom legislation in the form of Statutory Instruments (SIs) taking one or other of the various companies acts or other statutes as their authority have an all important effect on companies' responsibility for corporate governance generally and corporate actions in particular. Companies also have to comply with regulation emanating from the Financial Services Authority (FSA), such as the Combined Code on Corporate Governance. Increasingly, this legislation and regulation is itself subject to Europe-wide policies in the form of EU directives.

In the United States, corporation law is mainly a state matter so there can be variations from one US state to the next. However, the situation is made simpler by the fact that a large proportion of American companies are incorporated in the State of Delaware (the state allows out of state incorporations and does not tax trading activities that take place outside the state), so Delaware's General Corporation Law applies to a lot of US companies.[5] In addition, some 16 of the states conform to the Revised Model Business Corporation Act (1984) either wholly or substantially.[6]

---

[5] This is available on the web at: **http://delcode.delaware.gov/title8/c001/sc01/**. The general distinction between corporate governance, a state matter, and securities trading, a federal one, has become less clear cut since the passing of the Sarbanes-Oxley Act in 2002, the biggest incursion of federal power into corporate law since the 1930s. These variations between the states are more than cosmetic. For example, states like North Carolina would allow creditors to make claims against shareholders who had received 'excessive dividends', limited liability notwithstanding.

[6] These include Florida, Georgia, Indiana, Virginia and Washington.

Shaftesbury PLC, an AGM in practice

A look at Shaftesbury PLC, a property investment company in London's West End, gives a flavour of how one particular company's 2005 AGM altered the company's articles of association.

Among the changes to the company's articles of association proposed to the AGM in January 2005 were a proposal relating to uncertificated (ie, non-hard copy) shares, another allowing for electronic communication with shareholders, a third adjusting the rules for announcing changes to the time or place of a general meeting and a fourth altering (downwards) the amount of borrowing the directors could authorise without the specific authority of a general meeting of shareholders.

The explanatory notes make clear that the first two items comply with specific pieces of legislation.[7]

How big is the corporate action universe?

Before looking at particular types of corporate action, it is worth pausing for a moment to consider the sheer numbers of corporate actions taking place every year.

---

[7] Although company borrowing does not fall under the heading of corporate actions, technically speaking, and does not affect shareholders directly, as an alternative to share issues as a method of raising capital it merits the same kind of consideration by shareholders as real corporate actions. This area will be considered in more depth in the following chapter.

In 2004 the number of corporate actions taking place worldwide was estimated to be close to one million.[8] Given that each corporate action affects thousands of shareholders and that processing every corporate action involves several organisations in communicating and checking information, it will be clear that corporate actions administration requires huge effort and constitutes a complex industry. This industry is carried on away from the attention of the media, and the investor, for the most part. According to SWIFT the volume of corporate actions message traffic was 45 million in 2005, double the amount of 2002.[9] Completing corporate actions takes a lot of work and represents a substantial hidden cost for investors.

---

[8] 'Corporate Action Processing, What Are the Risks?' (Oxera, 2004) estimated that there were 935,200 corporate actions relating to equities that year, of which approximately two-thirds were North American and one-fifth European.

[9] Society for Worldwide Interbank Financial Telecommunication. Part of the increase is due to the recovery of stock markets from the bursting of the dotcom bubble. The volume of corporate actions normally peaks in May, reflecting the large number of corporate actions that take place in the spring results season.

2.

The Main Corporate Actions

A teeming universe of corporate actions

Estimates of the number of kinds of corporate action vary, partly because there are different definitions of what constitutes a discrete event and partly because new corporate actions are invented.[10] A conservative estimate of the number of types of corporate action would be around 70,[11] but others have put the total at over 150.[12] Thankfully, there are a small number of types of corporate action that are a long way out in front in terms of their importance, and this chapter will look at these in more detail.

Dividends

This must be the most familiar (and easily understood) corporate action of them all. It is also the most common type of corporate action – accounting for slightly less than 30% of all actions. A dividend is a distribution of cash to shareholders in proportion to their equity holding. No company is compelled to declare a dividend and those that do may vary the amount. Typically, a company will pay an interim dividend and a final dividend. The dividend is normally contingent on the approval of the AGM.

---

[10] For example, a rights issue is usually thought of as a single corporate action in terms of its import for the investor, but corporate action practitioners may see it as two separate actions; firstly, the distribution of the rights (nil-paid) and, secondly, the (call) payment for the new shares.

[11] 'Lost in Transcription' (The Banker, 1st June 2007).

[12] Infosys white paper (Ramamurthy, Arora & Ghosh, November 2005).

Some historical background on dividends

The modern use of the word dividend in English, as the share of the profit of a joint stock company, goes back to the early seventeenth century. The first companies paying dividends were the overseas trading companies such as the Dutch East India Company (the Vereinigte Oostindische Compagnie or VOC), which paid dividends varying between 12 and 75% a year in the seventeenth century. However, VOC shareholders did not always receive their dividends in cash; payments with VOC bonds or in kind (spices) also occurred, explaining why the shareholders were called the "pepper sacks of Amsterdam".[13]

The importance of dividends naturally varies from one company to another and there are also cultural differences in attitudes to dividends from one country to another. Generally speaking, dividends are more significant for shareholders in the UK than in other parts of the world, but the sad truth is that the long-term trend for dividends has been downwards, with the most marked decline occurring in the United States. The importance of dividends is always going to be relative to other factors. For instance, at a time when low rates of interest prevail, like the beginning of the current decade, company dividends will seem comparatively attractive. By contrast, when share prices are rising steeply the attractiveness of the dividend is likely to be overshadowed.

---

[13] These VOC dividend percentages are not true dividend yields based on the price the shares were trading at when the dividend was paid – in the early years of the 17th century there was no official quoted price with which to calculate a true dividend yield. Instead, the VOC dividend is expressed as a percentage of the price of the shares at issue (ie, their face value).

This, too, has been the state of affairs in the ten years to 2006 when dividends contributed just 8% of the total return to shareholders from their shareholdings. Changes to the tax regime of the shareholder may make it more advantageous for them to receive entitlements such as return of capital rather than dividends. However, in the UK share dividends are treated more favourably than income derived from other kinds of savings.[14]

Dividend yields

The size of the dividend is the key component of the dividend yield, one of the basic ratios used for evaluating shares and their price.

$$\text{Dividend yield} = \frac{\text{total dividend}}{\text{share price}}$$

Dividend cover

A tool for checking how affordable a dividend is by calculating how many times over the company could afford to pay the dividend out of its after-tax profits.

$$\text{Dividend cover} = \frac{\text{net profit}}{\text{dividend}}$$

---

[14] Chapter 9 looks at the tax implications of different kinds of corporate action in more detail.

Of course, in the long term every company must be able to afford its dividend and there are no guarantees that a company that has been paying high dividends might not to have to cut the dividend in the face of a drop in profits. Faced with this uncertainty, some investors rely on a company's dividend history as an indication of management skill and commitment to maintaining or (better still) consistently raising the dividend.[15]

Along with high rate deposit accounts, shares with a high dividend yield are a favourite among those (known as "income investors") who need to derive an income from their investments.

---

[15] *Money Observer* features its 'ten per cent club' annually. The UK companies listed have increased their dividends by 10% over 10 successive years.

Dividends – how they work in practice

Normally the announcements of the interim dividend and the final dividend will accompany the publication of half-year results and final results respectively. The following announcement would be typical:

Friday 14th March 2008

"The Board remains confident in the Group's earnings outlook and has decided to increase the final dividend by 5% to 25p per share. This brings the full year dividend to 39.9p per share, an increase of 5% on that paid for 2006. Going forward, the Board expects to grow the dividend gradually, while continuing to achieve greater dividend cover."

This would be followed by a timetable for the dividend payment:

Shares quoted ex-dividend[16]	28th March 2008
Record date	30th March
Final Dividend paid	21st May
The AGM	22nd May

---

[16] The ex-dividend date is the first day on which purchasing the shares would *not* entitle the investor to the dividend in question. The record date is the date on which the registrar would compile the list of shareholders due to be paid (these important dates are dealt with in more detail in the next chapter). Note that the approval of the final dividend payment would normally be the subject of a shareholder vote at the AGM, so the shareholders' approval is retrospective. If a company operates a dividend re-investment scheme they will normally make clear to shareholders the latest date for joining or exiting the scheme. In the above example a shareholder would know that they had to opt into the dividend re-investment plan by, say, 23rd April to be sure of having their final dividend re-invested.

Scrip dividends (paper instead of cash)

Whether the word scrip is derived from a scrap of paper or an abbreviation of subscription, the meaning is memorable enough; scrip dividends are an alternative of taking further shares in the company in place of a cash dividend.[17] A client will often be asked to decide as a matter of policy if they wish to receive scrip dividends (if offered) rather than the cash dividend when they first sign up with a stockbroker. However, ongoing arrangements like this are really a time saving convenience for the stock broking service and its clients; as far as the issuing company is concerned the shareholder normally has a choice between taking the scrip shares or the cash dividend. In the language of corporate actions they make an "election".

Scrip dividends are fairly common but by no means universal. For UK shareholders, receiving a scrip dividend has income tax implications.

Scrip dividends should not be confused with DRIPs (Dividend Reinvestment Plans) – arrangements for shareholders to have their dividend spent on the purchase of more shares in the company. The difference is that shares for a DRIP are bought on the stock market and the (small) charges are deducted to cover stamp duty and dealing costs. Using a DRIP facility is not a corporate action in itself, merely a service provided by some issuers once the dividend payment has been made.

---

[17] This description of 'scrip' is true in UK parlance. In the United States, the term 'scrip dividend' seems to be ambiguous and is sometimes used to describe a promissory note in lieu of an actual cash dividend. The term 'stock dividend' meaning a dividend paid in shares is also current in the US.

Scrip dividends in practice

Information about an issuer's policy on scrip dividends is generally available on the issuer's investor relations website. The issuer will require an instruction from the shareholder to confirm that they wish to receive their dividend in paper form. This could either be in the form of notification from the broker that this shareholder always opts for scrip dividends where they are available or a signed mandate from the investor that they wish this issuer's dividends in particular to be paid as a scrip dividend.

The ex-dividend date, record date and payment date for the scrip dividend will normally be the same as for the cash dividend.

The scrip dividend is normally calculated by means of a scrip dividend reference price, a divisor applied to the cash dividend entitlement to work out how many shares the cash dividend equates to. The scrip dividend reference price is calculated according to a formula such as the average of the middle market quotations for the issuer's shares on the five trading days commencing on the ex-dividend date.

Re-invested dividends

Over long time periods investors who can afford to re-invest dividends reap an enormous reward. For example, £100 invested in equities in 1945 would by 2007 have grown to £8511. However, with dividends reinvested, this figure would have been £131,369 – more than 15 times greater.

Performance figures for managed funds are normally on a dividends re-invested basis.[18]

---

[18] Barclays Capital Equity Gilt Study, 2005.

Scrip issues

Otherwise known as a *bonus issue* or a *capitalisation issue*, this is the issue of more shares to the shareholders in proportion to their existing shareholdings at no charge. The purpose of a bonus issue is normally to reduce a company's retained earnings (reserves) in proportion to its share capital.[19]

The effect of a bonus issue on the issuer's market capitalisation is to leave it (and the value of each shareholders' holdings) unchanged. The number of shares in issue goes up but the value of each share goes down. Normally, the dividend will be adjusted downwards to give the shares the same dividend yield as before.

For some markets (including the UK) the effect of reducing the price of individual shares can be advantageous as a very high price for shares is thought to put off investors.

In the US a scrip or bonus issue is known as a *share split*.

Scrip (bonus) issues in practice

A scrip issue will normally be put to the vote at a shareholder meeting before being put into effect. Practically, there is little a shareholder needs to worry about except to make a note of the date when the scrip issue is due to take place; otherwise the steep drop in the share price on the day in question may give them an unnecessary shock!

---

[19] Not to be confused with bonus share plans in Australia (which are covered in the glossary).

Normally, holders of physical share certificates will be issued with new certificates showing the new number of shares they hold, but shareholders should continue to keep the old certificate because proof of their shareholding is normally based on the old and new certificates together.

Return of capital

A *share capital reduction* is another name for this exercise. The effect of a return of capital is to leave the shareholder with cash compensation for ending up with fewer shares than they started with.

It is quite common for issuers to achieve a return of capital by replacing existing shares with a new share issue but, for example, only issuing four shares for every five held before. The shareholder will then receive a fifth 'B' share that can be cashed in at a future date.

Returns of capital accounts for 2% of all corporate actions.[20]

Share buyback – a non-event

Achieving a similar result as return of capital, a share buyback occurs when an issuer buys back its own shares on the open market.

---

[20] 'Corporate Actions Processing, What are the Risks?' (Oxera, 2004).

Normally a company would require the approval of a shareholder meeting for such a move but a share buyback is not a true corporate action. This is because the transaction takes place in the stock exchange rather than through formal contact with the shareholders about an entitlement that is proportional to their shareholding.

Both returns of capital and share buybacks have been fairly common in recent years as companies have tended to build up substantial reserves. Shareholders benefit directly from a return of capital while buybacks have an indirect benefit through the support to the share price of an issuer buying its own shares in significant amounts. Share commentators will often contrast actions like these with the launching of takeover bids, an alternative use for piles of cash.

However, share buybacks can be used by a company as a means of a (favoured) major shareholder increasing its holding. The share buyback by Arcelor in 2006 was controversial because the Severstal stake in the company would have risen from 32% to 38% of the shares.

Generally speaking, share buybacks usually result in a small initial increase in the share price. They can eat into a company's reserves of cash so there may not be funds for increased dividends straight away. Managements can be accused of trying to distract shareholders from poor performance with buybacks.

Shareholders with some capital gains tax allowance to spare mayprefer an issuer to spend its cash on share buybacks rather than on a higher dividend (which will be subject to income tax).

Consolidation

A share consolidation is the opposite to a share split or bonus issue, consisting of the replacement of the shares with a smaller number of shares with a higher face value.

There is no change to the issuer's market capitalisation, so in a one-for-two consolidation a shareholder would receive half the number of shares but the share price (as well as the face value) would be twice as great.

Rights Issues

One of the most important species of corporate action, rights issues are a method of raising more capital by issuing more shares to existing shareholders in proportion to their shareholdings. As with other share issues, rights issues have to be conducted according to the Listing Rules of the UK Listing Authority. The right to buy new shares in proportion to one's existing shareholding is known as a pre-emption right or subscription right and, in the UK, it normally requires a resolution to waive the right to be supported by 75% of shareholders.[21]

Clearly, only companies that need more cash will undertake such an exercise and rights issues are often interpreted as an important signal in the stock market. A rights issue confers an extra degree of influence to the shareholders as collectively they have power over the success or failure of the event. In the context of a rights issue, failure would be a widespread disinclination on the part of the shareholders to 'take up their rights' (pay for more shares in the company).[22] This not only sends

---

[21]However, there is an informal arrangement whereby the trade associations of the UK's institutional investors allow small issues of shares to be made that don't take account of shareholders' pre-emptive rights. Appendix III looks at the subject of pre-emptive rights and non-rights issues in more detail.

[22] This does not have to be an 'all or nothing' decision; shareholders are perfectly entitled to take up some of their rights but not all of them.

an important negative signal to the market about how shareholders feel about their company, but also means that the issuing company has to look to the open market for buyers of the newly issued shares. Big sale of shares naturally tend to have the effect of forcing the share price downwards.

Companies will normally offer the rights issue of shares to the shareholders at a discount to the current share price in order to encourage the level of take-up. A deeply discounted rights issue was at one time taken as an indicator of the management's lack of confidence and often heralded a decline of the company's share price. In recent years deeply discounted rights issues have become more frequent and investors tend to see them as no more than a strategy for ensuring that the rights are all taken up.

Shareholders and analysts will look beyond the corporate action to the 'narrative' coming from the issuing company. A rights issue to pay for a convincingly explained acquisition, for example, will find more favour than one launched by an insurance company that has just announced its reserves are insufficient to cover recent claims for hurricane damage. For companies with solvency problems a rights issue may be the only alternative to takeover or liquidation. In these circumstances the shareholders collectively hold the power to decide whether the company survives or not.

As with a company being listed on the stock exchange for the first time, an issuer launching a rights issue would normally use the services of an investment bank in a lead manager role. One of the tasks of a lead manager may be to underwrite the issue or arrange for it to be underwritten by other financial institutions, which means that they will buy the new shares of those shareholders who do not wish to take up their rights. Normally substantial fees are charged for underwriting, which accounts for the significant expenses of a rights issue (see the example below). [The role of the lead manager will be looked at in more detail in Chapter 4.]

FIBERNET GROUP PLC

4 FOR 15 RIGHTS ISSUE TO RAISE APPROXIMATELY £77.0 MILLION

INTRODUCTION

The Board announces a 4 for 15 Rights Issue of 12,826,325 New Ordinary Shares to raise approximately £75.7 million, net of expenses. The Rights Issue has been fully underwritten by Old Mutual Securities.

The Rights Issue is conditional upon, inter alia, Shareholders' approval which will be sought at the Extraordinary General Meeting.

The Rights Issue Price represents a 54.8%. discount to the closing middle market quotation of 1328 per Ordinary Share on 22nd November 2000, the last business day before this announcement.

Rights; tricky terminology

The key defining privilege for the existing shareholders in a rights issue is the opportunity to trade in the new rights issue shares when they are *nil-paid*, that is before having to pay for them.

Where there are no nil-paid rights to trade the issue is called an open offer but the existing shareholders still have subscription rights. Open offers are the norm in the United States. Sometimes the more helpful term *entitlement offer* is used.

The US and the UK also differ in a small but important variation in phraseology when it comes to these types of share issue. A US open offer might be expressed as a five for four issue, signifying that shareholders will have an entitlement of one extra share for every four already owned, so ending up with five shares. In the UK a rights issue in the same proportions would be expressed as a one for four issue of nil-paid rights.[23]

In some countries (including the UK) shareholders electing not to exercise their rights will receive a cash premium when the rights lapse. An arrangement like this is at the issuer's discretion. European practice is for the issuer (or lead manager) to tender lapsed rights automatically with the proceeds going to the initial holder of the right. Sometimes shareholders will use the money raised from the selling on of some of the rights to pay for the take up of the remainder.

---

[23] See Appendix III for more detail on pre-emption and alternatives for issuers. See also the phrase "excess application" in the Glossary of terms.

Takeover bids

Potentially, a takeover bid for a company in which you have a shareholding is the most significant corporate action of all. It can also be one of the most complicated and drawn out of corporate events, especially in instances where the bid is unwelcome to the directors of the prey or where a takeover battle develops with two (or more) predators fighting over the target company.

In the UK the regulating body is the Panel on Takeovers and Mergers, normally referred to as "The Takeover Panel", and takeovers have to abide by "The City Code on Takeovers and Mergers" (The Code).

'Triggers' along the way to a takeover

- The first hint of a takeover bid could be a stock exchange regulatory announcement that shares in the target company had been acquired by a rival or a private equity firm.

- Once the predator company (or companies acting 'in concert') have acquired 30% or more of the shares of the target company, the code requires them to make a 'conditional offer' for all of its shares. This offer is conditional upon enough other shareholders agreeing to sell their shareholdings for the predator to gain a controlling interest. Note that the offer must value the target company's shares at no less than the price paid by the predator in its most recent purchase of those shares.

- Once the predator has more than 50% of the shares, they have the power to out-vote any other shareholder. This is the point when, object achieved, their offer can become unconditional. However, the acquirer may postpone making the offer unconditional until they have agreements to sell that would

> bring their interest to as much as 75% of the voting shares or more. The predator company has a deadline of 60 days after the offer was announced for it to be made unconditional.
>
> - Once the predator has 90% of the shares the predator can buy up the remaining shareholdings compulsorily. At this point the target company's stock exchange listing ends.

While takeovers are often an opportunity for investors to make a profit on their investment, there are a number of potential drawbacks. A successful takeover could mean saying goodbye to a company with an excellent record for dividends. Indeed directors sometimes play on just that fact to foster shareholder loyalty, or they may decide to pay a *special dividend* in an effort to thwart a takeover (as happened in the takeover bid by MAN of Germany for the Swedish truck maker, Scania). If an acquiring company pays for the takeover by offering its own stock to the target company's shareholders, they may lose out if the merged companies fare badly after the takeover and the share price declines.

Where the shareholder may see pros and cons for the takeover bid, for the directors of the target company the situation is bound to be clear-cut and unwelcome. A hostile takeover bid can be an explicit or implicit claim that management of the predator company would make a better job of managing the target company than its current directors, who will, if the bid is successful, almost certainly be voted off the board.[24]

---

[24] Of course, there may be other arguments in favour of a takeover that don't reflect badly on the current management, for example, economies of scale or the desire of the acquiring company to gain access to the distribution channels of the target company. The subject of the long-term outcomes for mergers has been much researched and the view that only a minority are truly successful seems on the way to becoming orthodox.

A takeover bid presents the shareholder with three basic choices:[25]

1.   Accept the offer

2.   Reject the offer

3.   Sell their shares on the open market in the course of the bid. This option may be attractive in a situation where the shareholder is doubtful that the bid will be successful but wishes to take advantage of the (temporarily) increased share price that the bid has brought about. Alternatively, the offer may consist wholly or chiefly of shares in the acquiring company and the shareholder prefers to have cash straight away.

Takeover bids tend to be preceded by a period when rumours of bids abound and a subsequent stage when the intention to bid may be clear but the terms have not yet been announced.[26] Speculation about the price the predator may put on the target company's shares will be reflected in a higher (and possibly more volatile) share price at this time.

---

[25] Once a takeover has been successful a shareholder who did not accept the offer at the time has 'sell out' rights, the right to have their stake bought out by the new parent company. However, the acquirer will have "squeeze out" rights if their shareholding rises above a certain proportion (normally around 90% - EU law stipulates 90-95% but devolves the precise level to the decision of individual member states).

[26] See Chapter 3.

Poison pills

In some countries, it is common practice for companies to have "poison pills", which are designed to make hostile takeovers more difficult. Typically, this might mean that once a shareholder acquires as much as 15% of the voting shares in a company, all the other shareholders are able to buy new shares at a big discount to the stock market price. Poison pills have been upheld by the Supreme Court of Delaware until recently but this may be beginning to change. They also occur in Japan.

In recent years the idea of "chewable pills" has grown in favour. These are poison pills with features to make them more acceptable to shareholders, such as shorter lifespans or a triennial review of poison pills by independent directors.

Reverse Takeovers

A reverse takeover can mean the acquisition of a larger company by a smaller one, or the acquisition of a listed company by an unlisted one.[27]

Agreed takeovers

This kind of takeover (or merger) accounts for some of the most important takeovers, such as the acquisition of mobile phone operator O_2 by Telefonica of Spain.

---

[27] See Chapter 7.

Although an agreed takeover has a good chance of success, the shareholders should consider the reasons the target company's directors have for recommending the offer. For example, an agreed offer may arise where several predators are interested in the target but there is one that the directors of the target company prefer. Also, the acquiring company may have gained the support of (some of) the target's directors through offers of directorships in the merged company.

De-mergers

A de-merger occurs when a company spins off a business it owns into a completely separate company. This result is often achieved through an issue of shares in the de-merged entity to the shareholders of the original group (in proportion to their shareholdings).[28] The rationale for a de-merger may be that it permits each of the businesses to focus on their core activities or that the market capitalisations of the separate companies will become more than the market capitalisation of the original group, thus increasing shareholder value. To put it another way, it becomes clear that the original group is less than the sum of its parts.

For companies that are active in more than one kind of business, de-merger rumours can be a staple of comment by analysts and the financial press. This has been the case with Pearson, for example, which has divested itself of Royal Doulton, Madame Tussauds and its stake in Lazard Brothers and whose *Financial Times* subsidiary is a perennial favourite of de-merger speculation.

---

[28] Another form of de-merger would be a management buyout.

Severn Trent/Biffa, an example of how the sums worked out

Severn Trent's de-merger of its waste services subsidiary, Biffa, in the second half of 2006 was recommended to shareholders on the grounds that the two companies had few 'operational synergies' and that the de-merger would be an opportunity to return value to Severn Trent shareholders (who benefited from a return of capital and the receipt of shares in Biffa).

On 1st October 2006 a shareholding of 375 Severn Trent shares would have been worth £5,010. They would have received:

£618.75 as a special dividend (the return of capital)

375 new shares in Biffa (one for each Severn Trent share held)

250 new shares in Severn Trent (two for each three shares formerly held)

A year later (1st October 2007) the 375 Biffa shares were worth £833 and the 250 Severn Trent shares were worth £3,525, making a total of £4,408. If one adds back the special dividend the shareholder is slightly ahead.

But...!

For a higher rate taxpayer there would be some £155 in extra tax to pay on the special dividend.

3.

The Corporate Actions Process

Having looked at the main types of corporate action, this chapter will be dealing with how the processing of corporate actions appears from the point of view of the shareholder. Essentially, every corporate action comprises a few stages and the normal sequence is as follows:

1. Announcement date of the corporate action.

2. The ex-date – the first date on which shares are purchased without the entitlement of the corporate action in question.

3. Record date – the date at which the **registrar** extracts the list of holders of a particular stock from the **register** in order to process a corporate action.

4. Effective date of the corporate action.

In an ideal world, where all processes were instant, the ex-date and the record date would be the same. Although the processing of trades is a fraction of what it was 15 years ago, a time lag remains between share trades and share ownership information being passed to the custodian and the registrar/share register. Without some time elapsing between the two stages the anomaly of ex-shareholders appearing on the list of stockholders entitled to the corporate action would occur.[29] The key date for the investor is the ex-date. The investor may be unaware of the record date but it is pivotally important to those responsible for processing a corporate action, not least in investigating why a mistake has occurred in processing an event.

---

[29] This means that the opposite anomaly of actual stockholders missing out from a corporate action can happen instead. However, in the case of dividends, at least, the way it works seems fair.

Typically, in the UK the gap between the ex-date and the record date will only be a couple of days. However, there will normally be a much longer period between the record date and the effective date. A wait of seven or eight weeks from the record date is not uncommon and normally the intervening period will be at least a month.[30]

Corporate action processes vary in two main ways as far as the shareholder is concerned. Firstly, the kind of corporate action will affect the announcement date. Typically a dividend announcement, for example, will accompany the half-year (interim dividend) or final results (final dividend) but other corporate actions, such as a takeover bid, can be less predictable. Other corporate actions, such as a stock split, might be flagged as an intention when notice of the AGM is given but could just as well be the subject of an EGM. The formal announcement date for such a corporate action would be contingent on the shareholders approving the proposal at the meeting.

The second distinction from the point of view of the shareholder will be between those corporate actions requiring some kind of response from the shareholder (say, on whether they intend to take up their rights in a rights issue) and those that take effect automatically (such as a straightforward cash dividend).[31] In the latter case the sequence of stages listed above is adequate.

---

[30] Anyone who uses an online stockbroking service should be able to see an example of the delay in the gap between ex-dividend dates and payment dates. Ex-dividend dates normally fall on Wednesdays but dividend payment days vary.

[31] The corporate actions community tends to make a three-way distinction between compulsory (mandatory) actions, compulsory actions with options for the shareholders (such as scrip dividends) and voluntary actions (such as takeover offers).

Steps on the way to a takeover

Some of the customary developments in a takeover bid form a typical sequence. The list is by no means exhaustive and the chronological order can vary enormously:

- Statement of possible interest on the part of the (possible) predator

- Announcement by target company that an approach has been made to it

- **Shareholder letter from the target company to its shareholder** (normally letters of this kind include a clear warning to the recipient that "This document is important and requires your immediate attention")

- Announcement of the predator's definite intention to make a public offer for the target company's shares

- Statement that the target company has agreed to allow the predator a period for carrying out due diligence checks (normal in the case of agreed bids but not where the bid is hostile)

- Publication of the terms of the offer (including the closing date, which has to be at least 3 weeks after the publication – Day 21)

- Statement that the predator and the trustees of the target company's pension fund have agreed to exchange information

- Announcement by the predator on progress in gaining approval from regulatory bodies for the takeover

- Announcement of the proportion of the target company's voting shares that the predator has acquired (such announcements can appear on numerous occasions as the bid progresses)

- **Publication of offer documentation and commencement of offer period** (normally accompanied by the 'Form of Acceptance' for the shareholder to complete and instructions on effecting 'Electronic Acceptance' for those who hold their shares in Crest, and giving a first close date)

- Announcements by the predator company on its intentions relating to staffing levels, plant closures, head office closure or replacing the CEO in the target company in the event of the bid being successful

- **Announcement of revised takeover terms with a second close date** (this may occur no later than Day 46 of the bid under the City Code on Takeovers and Mergers)

- Announcement that the Minimum Acceptance Condition has been waived or altered (for example, a company might have set this at 75% of voting shares originally but later announce that it only requires 51% of the voting shares for its offer to go ahead)

- **Announcement by the predator that its offer has been declared "wholly unconditional" (this normally comes with figures on the number of shares and what percentage of the voting shares it has "acceptances" for)**

- **Announcements of the start (and end) of compulsory purchase of shares**

- Most of these announcements will be made by the announcements service of the stock exchange(s) where the target company's shares are listed. Items in bold would be formally notified to the holders of shares in the target company.

- Up until 39 days after the announcement (Day 39) the parties involved may release new information relevant to the takeover (eg, trading results).[32]

For actions that involve the shareholder in making a decision (an election) there may be many intervening stages between the announcement date for the event and its ex-date. The path of developments in a takeover bid, especially in a situation where the target company does not welcome the offer, or where there is more than one predator, is highly unpredictable. To take one recent example, The Royal Bank of Scotland/Banco Santander/Fortis takeover battle with Barclays Bank for ABN AMRO took over six months and included dozens of announcements from the contenders and the target before the RBS consortium offer became **unconditional.**

---

[32] A takeover bid is cumulative by nature so there is no single record date. The ex-date could be said to be the day after the offer closes. In the case of a failed bid there will be no effective date but where the bid is successful the effective date would be when the acquiring company fulfils the terms of its offer to the shareholders of the target company.

Spotting corporate actions data in the London Share Service

Notes	Price	Chng	52 week High	Low	Yld	P/E	Vol '000s
Alt Netwks ..†	134.50	–	177.50	129.50	2.8	10.1	11
AvantiCom ...	228.50	+2	267.50	.139	–	5.8	26
Getmobile Euro .q	120xd	–	160	92.50	7.3	6.9	5
Teleset	26.25	–	32	24.25	–	13.0	–

The London share prices in the *Financial Times* provide some essential facts for the benefit of the prospective investor.

The following symbols appear in the 'Notes' column:

s   Merger, bid or reorganisation in progress

†   Interim dividend since increase or resumed

‡   Interim since reduced, passed or deferred

P   Dividend adjusted for consolidation or share split

q   Earnings based on preliminary figures

These abbreviations can appear to the right of the share price:

xd   ex dividend

xc   ex scrip issue

xr   ex rights

xa   ex all (ie, without entitlement to current dividends, scrip issues or rights issues)

xR   ex capital distribution

Other corporate actions may be less complex than a takeover battle but still involve some interesting twists that distinguish them from the norm.

For example, a **return of capital** often involves the issuing of 'B' shares that can be redeemed for cash. In the case of the return of capital by Stagecoach PLC in 2004 the stages of this corporate event were as follows:

27th August	The AGM (which voted on the return of capital)
10th September	Last date for dealing in the existing ordinary shares
Same day after trading finished	Record time for the new (consolidated) ordinary shares and the redeemable 'B' shares
WEEKEND	
13th September	First day of trading in the new ordinary shares[33] & CREST accounts credited with new ordinary shares and 'B' shares[34]
15th September	Closing date for election to redeem or retain 'B' shares
22nd September	Despatch of cheques and crediting of CREST accounts in respect of those who elected for immediate redemption Despatch of share certificates for those who elected to defer the redemption of their 'B' shares Despatch of share certificates for the consolidated ordinary shares

A breakdown of the stages in the course of another important shareholder event, a rights issue, is also merited (as this is not a real-life example the stages are shown as days counting up to the

---

[33] In the case of an event like this where the existing ordinary shares were being swapped for consolidated ordinary shares it was imperative that no trading could be done in between the ex-date and the record date, which is why this stage of the corporate action would normally be timed to take place over a weekend.

[34] This event can be viewed as having two effective dates, the first when CREST accounts are credited with the consolidated ordinary shares and the 'B' shares, and the second on 22nd September with the despatch of cheques and share certificates and the crediting of CREST accounts.

commencement of dealing date, zero).[35] Note that for corporate action practitioners a rights issue is normally regarded as two distinct events; firstly, the distribution of the nil-paid rights and, secondly, the call payment when shareholders accept their new shares.[36]

-43	Prospectus in respect of 'one for one' rights issue
-32	Ex (rights) date[37]
-28	Record date for rights issue (and voting at the EGM called to vote on the proposal)[38]
WEEKEND	
-25	EGM approves rights issue Despatch of **provisional allotment** letters
-24	Commencement of dealing in new shares, nil paid Nil paid rights enabled in CREST[39]
-4	Latest time and date for **splitting** provisional allotment Letters, nil paid
-3	Latest time and date for acceptance and payment in full
-2	Latest time for registration of renunciation
0	Commencement of dealing in new shares **fully paid** Expected date for crediting rights issue shares to CREST stock accounts
+9	Certificated stocks despatched

---

[35] The rights circular will always include an 'Expected Timetable of Principal Events'. The Euroclear UK & Ireland website's Information Centre area includes a (model worded) sample of a rights circular (and a provisional allotment letter). As a rights issue is really two linked corporate actions "D day" can be either the day trading in nil-paid rights begins or the day that the trading of fully paid shares begins.

[36] 'Corporate Actions and ISO 15022 Standards: UK & Ireland Market Practice' (Securities Market Practice Group, Oct 2001, updated Aug 2004).

[37] Note that, as the ex date is before the shareholder vote, it is possible (though unlikely) that an investor could buy the shares "cum rights" only to have the proposal voted down at the EGM.

[38] Record dates for voting at shareholder meetings can be no more than 48 hours before the meeting, according to UK law. Most other jurisdictions allow a more generous amount of time to elapse (see Chapter 8 on shareholder voting).

[39] For the purposes of CREST nil-paid rights constitute a separate security from the existing shares and the fully paid shares that the nil-paid shares eventually become.

In passing, it is worth remembering that these stages merely track the life of a corporate action as it appears from the shareholder's viewpoint. The next chapter will look 'under the bonnet' to examine the processing of events more carefully. Suffice it to say that there is always the possibility of a processing error occurring. For example, a delay or failure to register a new shareholder who had purchased the share 'cum rights' could mean that they lost the opportunity to vote for the proposed rights issue at the EGM a few days later.

To predict the staging of any particular corporate action is no easy task, especially as there are so many hybrid events. In deciding the timetable of a corporate action the issuer is constrained by a number of imperatives; viz organising a shareholder vote, the time required for (clerical) processing, delays that need to be built into the timetable to allow for mail to be delivered and the rules of the stock exchange. In addition to all these, the shareholder needs a little time to read the prospectus, consult with a financial adviser and make up their mind. If shareholder 'thinking time' often seems unduly short, this is because of all the other factors the issuer (or the issuer's **lead manager**) has to take account of.

Chapter 7 looks at the issue of keeping informed about corporate actions in a timely fashion using the investor relations pages on company websites. Some companies make good use of their websites by posting helpful timetables for specific, complex corporate actions.

4.

The Corporate Actions Industry

What sort of animal are we talking about?

Having looked at the signs that the investor may be aware of as a corporate action progresses, this chapter will provide a view of what goes on behind the scenes. The (retail) investor is an outsider as far these processes are concerned, benefiting but not often involved.

The administration of corporate actions is a web of relationships spreading around the world. Although the reach of this network is international, the participants vary from one region to another.

Corporate actions processing is already heavily computerised and becoming more so. It is a rules based system but any description runs the risk of being misleadingly mechanistic if it ignores interventions by thousands of personnel, necessitated by the complexity of individual events.

Breaking down the complexity

It helps to imagine how a system for administering corporate actions would be organised if the need had only just arisen. In all probability, the system we would devise would comprise one giant computer storing all the data relating to all the shares issued and to whom they belonged. As a method of delivering entitlements to the right people it would be similar to a computerised system for administering social security payments or tax credits. The real-life corporate actions system differs from this model; it has evolved organically over many years to suit the interests of different parties. On the one side, for legal and historical reasons, the shareholder is assisted and represented by a trustee in the form of the **custodian**. On the issuer's side, the job of maintaining the **share register** of the issuing company is contracted out to a **registrar**.

Finally, complexity results from subtle changes in the relationships between the custodian (and custodian's nominee), the registrar, and the Central Securities Depository (CSD).

Let us take a look at the main components of the corporate actions processing machinery one by one.

Fig. 1 Model of the Main Participants in the Corporate Actions Process (United Kingdom)

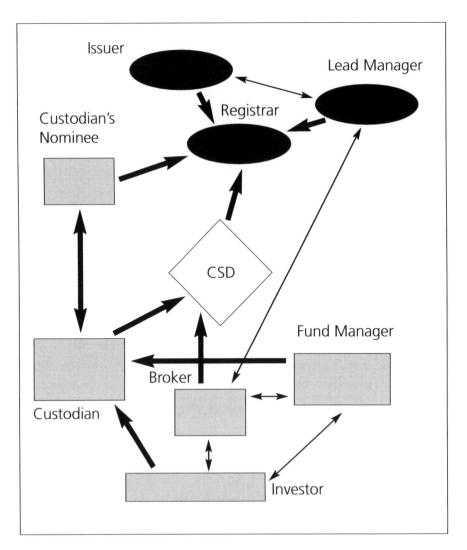

Key

Relates to the administration of shareholdings; passing information or devolving responsibility

Relates to the issuing / investing / dealing matters (ie, transactional)

CSD = Central Securities Depository

The shading is intended to distinguish those parties that work (directly) on behalf of the investor and those working on behalf of the issuer.

The Issuer

This is the company in its role as share issuer (and originator of corporate actions). Although maintaining good relations between a company and its shareholders effectively is vital to corporate success, as far as corporate actions are concerned, a company and its shareholders are separated by a chain of intermediaries.

The Share Registrar

Commercial companies that maintain the register of shares for quoted companies. The customary role of the registrar involved the cancellation and re-issue of share certificates as shares changed hands on the stock exchange. Registrars would normally be responsible for other registered securities (such as corporate bonds), a company's **treasury shares**, and administering **DRIPs** or employee share option schemes.

Contracting out the maintenance of the share register to another company is not a legal requirement but a cost effective way of discharging an important legal obligation.

Examples of registrars are Capita Registrars and Equiniti (formerly Lloyds TSB Registrars).[40]

Lead Manager – Investment Bank Financial Advisory Function

Lead management is a 'walk on' part in corporate action processing terms. Events such as a rights issues, for example, would probably involve the issuer in retaining the services of an investment bank to lead manage the issue.

One type of corporate action, mergers and acquisitions, is in a class of its own in terms of its importance to investment banks. When M&A is in vogue and investment banks are vying for a greater share of this business, the number and size of the deals in which they are involved is a matter of great significance for them. Investment banks' reputations in advising on other corporate actions have a much lower profile. The expertise in, for example, returns of capital or reverse takeovers, concentrated in investment banks will vary from one to another. However, this kind of detail is unlikely to be the subject of comment in the financial press when an issuer hires a new financial adviser (or corporate broker).

---

[40] In the USA in particular the companies performing the function of share registrar tend to be known as stock transfer agents.

Central Securities Depository

The Central Securities Depository (CSD) is the entity that comes closest to the single giant computer that we posited above. However, CSDs have only come into being in recent decades in order to avoid the business of share trading drowning in paperwork.[41] In terms of corporate actions CSDs have been superimposed on the existing system rather than entirely replacing it. The CSD is the organisation that holds the shares and carries out book entry transfers when the shares are bought and sold, a function that has encroached on the traditional role of share registrars in cancelling and re-issuing share certificates. The shares in the CSD may be in certificated form (traditional share certificates), albeit immobilised (ie, not needing to leave the CSD when there are changes of ownership), or de-materialised (in electronic form).

In the UK and Ireland the CSD is Euroclear UK & Ireland Limited. In the United States the Depository Trust and Clearing Corporation (DTCC) is the CSD. CSDs may be owned by a stock exchange, a central bank or increasingly, as in the case of Euroclear and DTCC, by a consortium of banks and other financial institutions.[42]

The categories of Euroclear membership include a 'personal membership' category for private investors.

---

[41] CSDs provide day-to-day clearing and settlement services for stock exchange trading.

[42] Appendix I is a list of central securities depositories.

(International) Central Securities Depositories, Historical Background

DTCC is the result of the 1999 merger of the Depository Trust Company (DTC) and the National Securities Clearing Corporation (NSCC). DTC's inception goes back to the late 1960s when the settlement of share trades on the New York Stock Exchange was causing a volume of paperwork that threatened to overwhelm broker's back offices. Government and regulators became concerned with the problem, which became so severe that the settlement period had to be increased from four days to five, T(rade) + 5.

Beginning in 1973, the DTC central depository overcame part of the administrative burden of settlement by locating share certificates in one place (the depository) and using book entries to record the changes of ownership, a process known as "immobilisation".

With the advent of electronic data the logical next step to immobilisation is "dematerialisation"; doing away with paper certificates completely.

Crest, the CSD for the UK and Republic of Ireland, was acquired by Euroclear in September 2002. Crest was created in 1994 and began settlements in August 1996. Euroclear acquired the French and Dutch CSDs in 2001 and 2002 respectively and in 2004 it went on to acquire the Belgian CSD.

Euroclear in the UK holds some but not all shares in dematerialised form. Dematerialisation has been completed for France, Belgium, the Netherlands and Ireland. An earlier attempt to bring about dematerialisation, the Taurus project, was abandoned in 1993 owing to cost overruns and flaws in its conception. At the time the failure of Taurus represented a serious knock to London's prestige as international financial centre.

The pivotal role of CSDs on the corporate actions stage was not part of their original *raison d'être*. They owe their existence to the enormous increase in securities trading in recent decades and the need to increase the efficiency of the trading settlement process.

An International Central Securities Depository is a CSD providing clearing and settlement facilities for cross-border transactions in domestic securities and/or international securities transactions.

The world's third ICSD is Clearstream, part of Deutsche Börse.

Custodian (& Custodian's Nominees)

A financial institution that holds shares and other securities and assets in safe keeping for investors, both institutional and private. Often the custodian will be a separate arm of the investment manager institution. The shareholdings are held through the **custodian's nominee** to keep the **beneficial owners'** holdings separate from the interests of the custodian company. To give an idea of the scale of custodial services, in 2001 Euroclear (known as CREST at the time) reported that 1,400 nominees were participants.[43]

---

[43] "Moving towards a Dematerialised Securities Market", CREST consultation document, July 2001.

It is important to understand that the use of a custodian is not universal. Private/retail investors who have Euroclear personal membership will not be using the services of a custodian and neither will private shareholders who continue to hold their stocks in certificated form.

Custodians hold accounts with the Central Securities Depository and normally have service level agreements to fulfil with fund managers or investors.

Refinements in custody

- Our model of the main players in corporate actions is good for a single country's stock market but in reality one fund manager may have investment funds covering many markets around the globe. The custody needs of these wide-ranging investments are met by **global custodians**, such as The Bank of New York Mellon or State Street Bank. Customarily, the global custodian may devolve custody of securities traded in a foreign market to a **sub-custodian** who is a participant in that country's Central Securities Depository. Sub-custodians are not necessarily only active in one country; HSBC, for example, provides sub-custody services in markets right across the Middle East and Asia. Custodians are sometimes known as **agent banks**.

- Some issuers provide their own nominee service as a **corporate nominee**. Examples of this approach occurred during the demutualisations in the UK financial sector in recent years such as that of the Bradford & Bingley Building Society in 2000. As a device to facilitate the issue of shares in a single company's stock, it clearly has its merits. However, it would be cumbersome when it came to administering share portfolios comprising stock in different companies.

The Investor

The investor may be investing directly or through an institutional shareholder such as an investment fund or life assurance company. Most of these institutions have their own fund managers but some have the work done for them by an outside team of fund managers. In the case of investments made through an institutional shareholder the retail client has no involvement in the corporate action process whatsoever.[44] The link from the investor to the custodian in figure 1 only applies to retail (private) investors buying shares though a broker (often with a financial adviser as an intermediary).

Fund managers all have 'back office' functions dealing with matters such as settlement, records, regulatory compliance and, of course, corporate actions. Once again, this function may be in-house or contracted out to a specialist.

Broker

For the purposes of this model "broker" can mean a stockbroker function performed on behalf of a fund manager or for private clients and includes online share trading services and services provided through a financial adviser. Our model does not show a direct connection between the broker and the custodian as the latter's primary obligation is to the shareholder. However, most stockbroker services will either have an in-house custodian/nominee service or a relationship with one provider of custodian services.[45]

Brokers have accounts with the Central Securities Depository and service level agreements with fund managers.

---

[44] The same is also true of multi-manager funds (sometimes known as 'funds of funds'); the multi-manager fund has no direct corporate action entitlements or involvement with the corporate actions process.

[45] Transact Nominees is one example of such a provider of custodian services.

What happens when a corporate action occurs?

Having described the parts of the corporate actions machine, let us now move on to describing the processing of a corporate event.

The deciding factor for the processing of an action is the way in which the investor holds their shares. The "form" of the shareholding determines the route by which the corporate action entitlement will flow from the issuer to the beneficial owner.[46] The main ways of holding shares (all mentioned already in this chapter) are the following:

- in certificated form

- through a custodian's nominee

- through a corporate nominee

- as a personal member of Euroclear (or another CSD)

In terms of the value of holdings the use of a custodian is overwhelmingly the most important as this is the normal way in which institutional investors' holdings are managed.

The existence of multiple routes for the corporate action to reach the beneficial owner means that the share registrar, the CSD, custodians, fund managers and financial advisers can all be involved in processing the same corporate action in parallel or one after the other. The stages that each must follow, once the corporate action data has been communicated by the issuer (or the issuer's lead manager), are as follows:

1. Capture and cleansing of the terms of the corporate action (ie, making sure that the information has been properly received and understood – this is often referred to as **data scrubbing**).

---

[46] It would be perfectly possible for the same corporate action entitlement from one company to reach an investor by two or more routes, if, for instance, a private investor held some shares in a company in certificated form and shares in the same company through a discretionary dealing account with a stockbroker (and hence using the services of a custodian).

2. Determining the entitlement (high up the chain, identifying the beneficial owner of a share may not be possible so, where the shares are held through an **omnibus nominee**, the registrar or CSD would only be able to determine who the custodian was and pass on to them the responsibility for identifying the ultimate owner).

3. Communicating the corporate action information.

4. Calculating resultant entitlements.

5. Disbursing the entitlements (otherwise known as "event settlement").

6. Reconciliation.

Naturally, in those cases where the beneficial owner is required to make an election[47] the sequence will become more complicated with the communication of the choices to the shareholders and the latter's elections being passed back up the chain.

None of the parties involved in processing corporate actions are obliged to guarantee the accuracy of the information they are passing down to the next link in the chain. Consequently, data scrubbing has to be undertaken at each stage of the processing of a corporate action, a feature of the corporate actions industry that the next two chapters will look at in more depth.

Can it all be done under one umbrella?

With the exception of the role of Central Securities Depository, some or all of the protagonists on the corporate actions stage can be the same player wearing different hats. Major banks often have different arms providing services in the areas of broking, fund management, lead management, custody and share registration. The possibility of conflicts of interest arises and comes under the scrutiny of financial regulators.

---

[47] See Chapter 3.

Fig. 2 Fingers in pies: A European bank

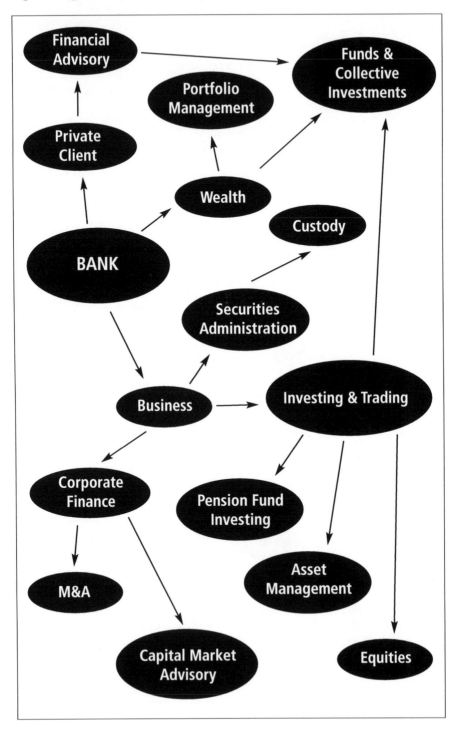

The Legal Framework

In the UK the responsibility for safeguarding share certificates and the administration of corporate actions are a regulated activity under the Financial Services and Markets Act 2000. Any player in the corporate actions industry who exercises any degree of discretion in their administration will also come under the regulated activity of managing investments. In both cases the regulator is the Financial Services Authority (FSA).

In the USA the law applying to corporate actions is in Title 15, Chapter 2a of the United States Code and the regulator is the Securities and Exchange Commission (the SEC).

The machinery for processing corporate actions can on occasion be put to other uses. Thus, information to shareholders about bankruptcy proceedings may travel along the same lines of communication. Information on class action litigation by shareholders is another example of non-corporate action use that the system can be put to, and the resulting award may reach the investor along the same route as a corporate action entitlement release.

5.

How Well is the Corporate Actions System Working?

'This is, after all, one of the most collaborative of industries.'[48]

'The fiduciary responsibility that I have to my own clients dictates that I will do all in my power to ensure that somebody else bears responsibility for any material losses that occur.'[49]

There is more than one way to judge the success of corporate actions processes. The routine cost of corporate actions to the investment industry, and ultimately to the investors themselves, is one very important gauge of how fit for purpose the system is. However, in addition to running costs, it is also worthwhile to identify the size and location of potential risks when things go wrong.

Costing corporate actions

Putting a figure to the worldwide cost of processing corporate actions is not easy but there is scope for estimating the system's running expenses relative to the values of stock under custody.

Since the stock markets started to recover from the dotcom bubble there has been a steep rise in the number of corporate actions with the volume reported to have doubled since 2003.[50] Soon the number of corporate actions relating to shares will reach the two million mark.[51]

The world's largest Central Securities Depository, the Depository Trust & Clearing Corporation of the US (DTCC), had $36 trillion worth of

---

[48] James Femia, MD Depository Trust and Clearing Corporation, addressing the International Securities Industry Practitioners Symposium, London 24 May 2004.

[49] 'Managing Risk in Corporate Actions: How far has the industry come?' published by Financial Services Research, April 2006, volume Q2 2006, pp 34-45.

[50] Corporate-Actions The Power of Technology, FTSE Global Markets November/December 2006.

[51] This figure is exclusive of scheduled fixed interest payments relating to bonds, whose volume far exceeds the corporate actions relating to equity.

securities on deposit (approximately €27.25 trillion at the time), according to its 2006 Annual Report. The company reported that the 2006 corporate actions it processed were worth $3.3 trillion,[52] which involved data scrubbing of 900,000 separate events. Revenue from custody services was approximately $210 million.

In 2004 the value of assets under custody with the world's 41 largest global custodians was in the region of €46 trillion with the custody services of State Street Bank, the leading global custodian, accounting for €7.9 trillion.[53] State Street remains the world's leading global custodian with approximately €9.5 trillion of assets under custody in June 2007. Extracting information on a bank's revenue relating to corporate actions can be difficult but State Street's second quarter 2007 figures showed that 'servicing fees' contributed $766 million (approximately €550 million) to income.

The leading UK global custodian is HSBC Global Investor Services, which had €1.1 trillion of assets under custody in 2004, rising to just under €3.5 trillion by the end of 2006.[54] For 2006 income from its global custody operation was approximately €600 million.

Although all the parties involved in processing a corporate action will charge for their part in the chain linking the issuer to the investor, these figures for individual participants go some way to demonstrating that the costs involved are dwarfed by the value of the cash benefits to the investors, let alone the size of the underlying investments.

---

[52] The DTCC Annual Report does not give a breakdown between corporate actions relating to equity and those relating to fixed interest securities.

[53] 'Corporate Action Processing, What are the Risks?' (Oxera, 2004).

[54] In fact, HSBC's importance in custody terms arises chiefly from its leading position in Asia and the Middle East; it is the leading sub-custodian in the majority of these markets.

Where do the costs arise?

Identifying the costs of processing corporate actions to custodians and other players is even more difficult than calculating the income they derive from the work. The first major cost arises from staffing for work that requires intelligence and sound judgment and where experience is at a premium. Corporate action jobs command salaries at the top end of the range for workers in 'middle office' roles. That said, corporate action teams tend to be small with over 50% of custodians having teams with no more than 10 staff.[55]

Secondly, corporate action players often subscribe to multiple sources of information in order to protect themselves from missing a corporate actions announcement (see text box below). Naturally, checking all this data means more work for the corporate actions staff to do. No one party involved in processing corporate actions guarantees the information supplied to any other party, with the result that corporate action data constantly needs to be re-checked. This factor acts as a drag on the efficiency of the system as a whole at the expense of the investor.

---

[55] Corporate Actions Automation Survey, 2003 (CityIQ).

Corporate Actions Data Sources

Information Providers:

Bloomberg

EActions (a service of Hub Data)

Exchange Data Int'l. (publisher of the Corporate Actions Bulletin)

FT Interactive data

Reuters (providers of the DataScope service)

Standard & Poor's

Telekurs Financial

Thomson Financial DataStream

Exchange/Central Securities Depository Sources:

London Stock Exchange Corporate Action Diary service

DTCC Global Corporate Action Validation Service (GCA)

Tokyo Market Information Service

Finally, the corporate actions industry faces significant costs in improving automation of processes. Chapter 6 will look at the technological challenges facing the industry in more depth. Suffice it to say that investment in automating corporate actions will probably reach the €1bn mark in the current decade.

Expenditure on corporate actions processing and investment by industry participants are both dependent upon the overall prosperity of the investment industry in general, and the continued increase in the volume of corporate actions in particular.

The cost of corporate action mistakes

No list of the costs facing corporate actions processing would be complete without taking into account exceptional expense arising from mistakes being made. Risk is an important consideration for the corporate actions community and participants have demonstrated an increasing awareness of the threats that they face.

The G30 set the tone in 2003, when it turned its fire power on event processing with the conclusion that 'corporate Actions, across the market, are the major source of financial losses attributable to operational failure.'[56] The risks of corporate actions systems failures are disproportionately high in relation to the routine costs of corporate actions processing. This is at odds with the industry's normally low profile. The greatest danger is that event processing errors will cause missed trading opportunities (or ill-advised trading) when decisive shifts in share price are taking place.

---

[56] G30's 'Global Clearing and Settlements - Plan of Action' (2003). The Group of Thirty (G30) is a private, non-profit, international body composed of senior representatives of the private and public sectors and academia. An earlier study ('Risks and Regulation in European Asset Management: Is there a Role for Capital Requirements?', J. Franks, C. Mayer & Oxera, 2001) found that fund management firms rated corporate action failures as the third highest operational risk.

Missing the boat...an example of losses arising in a takeover situation

A potential corporate actions processing mistake that has been cited as an example in the past is a mix up over a client's instructions in a takeover situation. The takeover offer is wholly comprised of shares in the acquiring company. The client intends to accept the offer and instructs their broker to this effect but the broker mistakenly sells the clients shares in the target company on the open market. In the time it takes for this error to be reported the predator company's shares rise in value considerably, a turn of events that the investor had predicted and hoped to benefit from.

In this scenario the broker is liable for the consequences of this mistake. The broker will have to purchase the same number of predator company shares on the open market as their client would have received if they had accepted the offer on the client's behalf. The broker will sustain a substantial loss in this case. Of course, it is possible that the predator company's shares might have decreased in value after the mistake was made, but then it is less likely that the client would have insisted on the situation being put right!

Operational risks in actions processing remains a major hazard and mitigating the danger adds to the costs of the industry. The size of the threat is impossible to gauge as, for understandable reasons, participants in the corporate actions chain are loath to own up to being affected by these kinds of mistake.

One exception to the general silence on the subject of mistakes and risks was the report by the Swiss CSD, SegaInterSettle (SIS), in its report 'CloseUp – Corporate Actions; Risks? – a quantitative study.' For 2004 this study published the following findings:

> Cash-related corporate actions (dividends etc.)
>
> Value of all corporate actions   SwFr 162,800,000,000
>
> Total settlement losses   SwFr 72,908
>
> Mandatory actions with options & voluntary actions
>
> Value of all corporate actions   SwFr 197,800,000,000
>
> Total settlement losses   SwFr 682,618

Moving on from actual losses to put a scale on potential losses, the study estimated that the worst case scenario that SIS needed to allow for was a loss of SwFr 20m, and indicated that the organisation would use indemnity insurance to protect itself in the event of a loss of this size occurring. However, it is important to remember that this is the risk for just one part of the global corporate actions system and that other players, notably fund managers and brokers, face much greater risks. Not unreasonably, SegaInterSettle has suggested that other participants in the industry might share in their efforts to quantify the financial risk of making mistakes.

The SIS study confirms the general view that plain mandatory events such as dividend payments are the type least prone to errors in processing (although shareholders may be affected by payment delays, especially in the case of securities issued in developing markets). Interestingly, the study identified a correlation between costs arising from mistakes and the number of corporate actions, but no link with the settlement volumes (the size of a corporate action in terms of the number of shares affected by it).

Different components of the corporate actions industry may be the cause of problems or be impacted by them to different degrees.

Issuers

Issuers and their lead managers have it in their power to make life more difficult for other participants in the corporate actions process through the complexity of corporate actions that they initiate. Newly evolved corporate actions, ones that create complex tax situations or simply fail to communicate information in accepted standard language, can all cause complications for other players.

It is also not unknown for issuers to make basic mistakes in communicating corporate actions. For example, the UK Listing Authority took issuers to task in its September 2006 newsletter for submitting corporate action information to Euroclear that differed from the information shareholders had received in prospectuses.

Central Securities Depositories

CSDs will always clear up issuers' mistakes but custodians (and other CSDs) are not normally able to negotiate the level of care they receive from a CSD. CSDs do not guarantee the accuracy of the information they provide on corporate actions, so the next party in the corporate actions chain will need to do their own checking. (The reliability of corporate actions information is generally not guaranteed; vendors/providers may evidence robust procedures for checking their data but will normally stop short of full liability in the event of errors.)[57]

---

[57] In 2005 DTCC recorded 5,825 post payment date adjustments for interest and dividends payable on all the instruments it serviced, except collateralised mortgage obligations or asset backed securities, making an adjustment rate of 0.2% ('Structured Securities Processing Challenges', DTCC, June 2006).

Custodians

Global custodians may be vulnerable to mistakes in processing by the sub-custodians that they contract with for services in overseas markets. In turn **sub-custodians** are subject to the standards of the Central Securities Depository in their market.

Generally speaking, the more fund managers and institutional investors a global custodian provides services to, the greater would seem to be the risk of processing failures.[58] They are vulnerable because of the volume of assets they have under custody and because more clients equates to more work.

Custodians are tending to tighten up contract terms with their clients. For example fund managers who miss deadlines for passing back instructions to their global custodian may be issued with a "no response" notice. This is the corporate actions equivalent of "too late, mate".

With demanding clients and non-negotiable levels of quality of service from depositories, it looks as if the custody business feels pressure on both fronts. The recognition that there are risks in the business of custodianship is borne out by the existence of firms like Thomas Murray who specialise in evaluating and rating custodial (and depository) risks.

Fund Managers

It has been argued that broker dealers and asset managers are the industry participants with most to lose from mistakes in corporate actions processing and, therefore, that they have set the pace when it

---

[58] 'Corporate Action Processing, What are the Risks?' (Oxera, 2004).

comes to improving the flow of information.[59] However, asset managers have sometimes been slow in the take-up of new technology; it is still common for clients' instructions to be passed back to custodians by fax. It is also common for hedge fund managers to test the limits in delaying issuing their instructions to custodians.

The risks fund managers and brokers face in relation to corporate actions are generally similar to the example given above of a takeover situation where a share-trading mistake is made. One study has said that the trading risks for fund managers or brokers, arising out of corporate actions, is €1.5bn or higher each year.[60] Fund managers also face the lesser (but still significant) risk of the wasted transaction costs of misinformed trading. Trading on poor corporate action information is likely to be a problem for some fund managers but not all, so some investors are destined to lose out more than others.

In the end, who pays the cost of mistakes?

In instances where an investor's explicit, timely instructions have been mistakenly interpreted the likelihood is that the broker will compensate for their mistake. When a fund manager makes a poor trading decision based upon a faulty interpretation of information about a corporate

---

[59] Amy G. Harkins, senior vice president and director of global asset servicing for Mellon Financial made this point in FTSE Global Markets, November / December 2006. However, when it comes to corporate actions technology, awarding the dunce's cap is controversial with Wall Street and Technology ('Asset Managers Adopt a Software-as-a-Service Model for Corporate Actions Processing', December 2007) arguing that the volume of corporate actions work carried out by custodians resulted in them being ahead of fund managers in automating their processes.

[60] 'Corporate Action Processing, What are the Risks?' (Oxera, 2004). The Oxera study estimates that each year there are some 18,000 (complex) corporate actions affecting shares on the world's leading 25 stock exchanges. These corporate actions have the potential to lead to trading mistakes. The Oxera study puts the risk in the range of €1.5bn to €8bn, but the calculations are dependent upon a number of assumptions around the average price impact of actions and the timescale over which the price range occurs.

action, the investment fund, pension fund or investment trust will be the poorer for it. To outsiders these mistakes will be indistinguishable from other poor trading decisions that contribute to the fund managers overall performance rating.

There are comparatively few fund managers with reputations that have survived for decades; given the chanciness of investing, this is hardly surprising. However, share trading that arises out of corporate actions is one area where well-informed decisions should always be possible. Indeed, some fund managers employ front office teams specialising in share trades based on the scope for arbitrage when corporate actions take place. It is difficult for retail investors to spot which investment funds are developing their corporate actions expertise but, hopefully, financial advisers will become more aware of the importance of sound event interpretation and advise their clients accordingly.

In summary

Cooperation and liaison are vitally important to the corporate actions industry but the different players are individually accountable to their clients/participants for mistakes. To that extent, the current state of affairs falls short of full collaboration. The aggregate cost of corporate actions processing is low in proportion to total investments or sums accruing to investors from corporate actions.

Michael Kempe, a Euroclear director and Chairman of a European Central Securities Depository Association (ECSDA) working group, has said that firms involved in corporate actions have almost completed identifying risk and mitigating against it in their domestic markets (although there are still dangers when corporate action processes span national frontiers).[61] Nevertheless, through automation and

---

[61] From 'Managing Risk in Corporate Actions: How far has the industry come?'.

standardisation, there is potential for further reductions in costs and risks. The next chapter will look at areas where progress can be made and the question of whether it will take greater collaboration or stronger regulation to bring this about.

6.

Corporate Actions; Technology and the Future

How thoroughgoing does change need to be?

Although the problems of costs and risk are not terminal threats facing the corporate actions industry, in order for the tide of automation to be of real benefit, radical re-engineering of the system has been required. The case for investment in automation has relied on predictions of increasing cost and increasing risk arising from a greater volume and complexity of corporate actions. Participants' reactions have been dictated mainly by their assessment of the dangers (and rewards) that they face individually. The best solutions to the problems of processing corporate actions would be industry-wide ones but, because the decisions to invest in automation are made unilaterally, the result has been piece-meal improvements.

The most significant advances made to date could be characterised as a framework for change rather than a corporate actions revolution. Nevertheless, there has been no shortage of discussion on automation and standardisation.

Engaging in the debate on these subjects is a measure of an individual player's recognition that corporate actions are more than just a by-product of their other activities, be they securities broking, fund management or trade settlement.

A starting point

In the dense jungle of working groups, reports, white papers, conferences, trade journal articles, and product releases that have addressed the need for improvements to corporate actions processes one development stands out head and shoulders above the rest in significance: the introduction of **ISO 15022**, the international standard for electronic messages exchanged between securities industry players.

The moving force behind the creation of the new standard was SWIFT (The Society for Worldwide Interbank Financial Telecommunication), the body that sponsored the application for a new standard to the ISO shortly before the millennium. SWIFT's own messages were switched over to ISO 15022 from 2002 and SWIFT became fully ISO 15022 compliant in May 2003. SWIFT continues to have a sponsoring role for the standard as its registration authority, and each November it publishes enhancement releases for ISO 15022, maintaining and extending its usefulness for sending corporate actions messages.

Message Type	Used for
MT564	Notification message for a corporate action with details including options and possible entitlements
MT565	(owner's) instruction message – ie, in the case of mandatory actions with options or voluntary actions.
MT566	Confirmation message – that cash or securities have been credited to, or debited from, an account as a result of a corporate action
MT567	Status and processing advice request – used to advise on the status, or a change in the status, of an action for which the shareholder has already made their election
MT568	Corporate action narrative for complex instructions

The main corporate action message types under ISO 15022 (there are many more message types within ISO 15022 relating to other matters such as trading, settlement and securities lending).

SWIFT (ISO 15022) messages for a typical cash dividend

1. Preliminary information (MT564)

2. Complete information (MT564, again)

3. Entitlement calculation (MT564, and again)

4. Payment of cash dividend (MT566)

and for a rights offer

1. Announcement of the rights offer (MT564)

2. Notification of entitlement at ex-date (MT564)

3. Shareholder's instruction (MT565)

4. Status of processing instruction (MT567)

5. Notification of shareholder's entitlement at the deadline date (MT564)

6. Payment of shares or cash or both (MT566)

SWIFT has been keen to remind its participants of the cost reductions that using ISO 15022 has permitted and many important participants in the corporate actions system have added weight to the view that standardised corporate action messages are the key to automation. This in turn will lead to greater efficiency, increased speed and decreasing costs. The phrase Straight Through Processing, normally abbreviated to STP, is used repeatedly as shorthand for the changes the corporate actions industry needs to undergo. Turning ambitions for STP into practice has been slowed by a number of factors facing industry players small and large.[62]

---

[62] STP is also a catchword in areas such as clearing and settlement, and just because an institution is an STP leader in one area it does not necessarily follow that the achievement applies to all areas.

Problems along the way

Most industry participants seem agreed that the biggest stumbling block has been the widespread failure by issuers to standardise their event notifications right at the beginning of the corporate actions process. Although standardising corporate actions may not loom large for issuers, they will often be taking advice on corporate action design from lead managers or capital market advisory teams. These people work for the very same organisations whose custody and asset management departments are caused such problems by non-standard actions messages further along the chain. No efforts to bridge this disconnection have been publicly reported and the current mainstream view is that issuers will only be brought into line by regulatory action preventing them from "polluting" the headwaters of the corporate actions process.[63] To be fair to issuers (and their agents), they could claim that standardisation, rather than making things simpler for everyone, gives their staff extra complexity to cope with.

In the UK, the enforcer of standardised notifications for corporate actions would be the UK Listing Authority. To protect investors, the Listing Rules mandate what announcements companies must make but the authority has no responsibility for ensuring the smooth running of corporate actions processing. Standardised notifications could be seen as creating a novel constraint on corporate investor relations.

Merely making use of the ISO 150022 standard by no means guarantees that STP will flourish. Many industry participants have problems in the correct drafting of ISO 15022 messages, especially when it comes to classifying the corporate action. There is not even a unified, universally

---

[63] DTCC has campaigned for the SEC to require issuers to use standard templates for corporate actions (cf, 'Transforming Corporate Action Processing', 2003). The Association of Global Custodians (AGC) has called on its member banks to encourage their issuers' agent operations to standardise their announcements ('Statement on the Need for Universal Standardized Messaging in Corporate Actions', June 2007).

accepted system for the identification of the securities the corporate actions relate to.[64]

Evidence of problems with standardisation in the field include DTCC's revealing in 2006 that in the 1,500 to 3,000 MT564 and MT568 messages it was receiving each week at that time, the fourth largest category of corporate actions was "unknown". This means that the description of the corporate action would need to be read and interpreted by a member of staff, thus causing a snag in the straight-through processing. The extent of the complexity in corporate actions that ISO 15022 allows for is a matter for some debate, but SWIFT argues that all it usually needs is for a complex event to broken down into its constituent elements.[65]

Even within a single organisation committed to using ISO 15022, there can be varying practices in corporate action messaging. Mellon Financial, for example, discovered that staff in Asia, Europe and North America had differing views on the correct way of completing an MT567 message.

Let there be standards

The biggest impetus for standardisation of corporate actions across markets has come from the European Union, in particular the 2006 Giovannini Protocol. The protocol calls for standard automation technologies to be put in place by all EU market participants by 2011. It arose out of the Giovannini Groups reports on European clearing and settlement arrangements (published in 2001 and 2003), which identified corporate actions processing as the third barrier, of fifteen, to harmonisation.

---

[64] Vendors of corporate action data and processing systems normally have to incorporate ISIN and SEDOL codes and, where necessary, identifiers that have currency in local markets.

[65] Catherine Marks, quoted in 'Managing Risk in Corporate Actions: How far has the industry come?' (Financial Services Research, April 2006).

Automation does equal greater efficiency: reports from the field

- JPMorgan, the third largest global custodian, has been using Xcitek systems for processing corporate actions since the start of the decade (and was the first SWIFT participant to accept ISO 15022 corporate actions messages). They reported a three-fold increase in the volume of events processed while staff levels increased by less than one percent.

JPMorgan has been an advocate of providing links in corporate action messages to prospectuses in PDF format in the case of events such as rights issues or takeover offers.

- SegaInterSettle (SIS), the Swiss CSD, was able to make a reduction in personnel as a result of a process-oriented (re)organisation and the introduction of Corporate Actions Enhanced Services (CAES), a web product designed to process events.

Clients using CAES can avail themselves of templates for corporate action letters in English, French, German or Italian to send to their own clients with editable fields in which to insert their own recommendations or choices.

- Northern Trust, another top 10 global custodian, used ISO 15022 in automating communications and as of 2006 99% of its corporate action messages to and from agents were automated. Fund manager clients who use automated messaging like SWIFT's are given longer deadlines for elections and Northern Trust will coach clients on the correct formatting of messages.[66]

---

[66] Details taken from **www.xsp.com**, JPMorgan Securities submission to 'The Asset Managers Forum Corporate Actions Initiative' (November 2006), 'Risks? – A quantitative study' (SIS, January 2006), The CAES brochure published by SIS, and 'Managing Risk in Corporate Actions: How far has the industry come?' (Financial Services Research, April 2006).

At the same time as the Giovannini Group was deliberating, the problems of corporate action processing were also being looked at by the European Central Securities Depositories Association (ECSDA) ISO 15022 and the Securities Market Practice Groups (**SMPGs**). The latter in particular, covering around 30 markets in the Americas, Asia and Europe have undertaken detailed analysis of what was required of corporate action messaging in their individual markets and the best way to use ISO 15022 to implement those standards. Thus the UK and Ireland SMPG produced practice guidelines on corporate actions and ISO 15022 as long ago as October 2001, before SWIFT began generating ISO 15022 messages. The UK and Ireland guidelines (which were updated in August 2004) are among 14 such documents produced by SMPGs.

The pinnacle of the SMPG's achievement has been the **Event Interpretation Grid**, often referred to as just "the grid", which aims to promote harmonisation between different markets when it comes to corporate action messaging.[67] The grid, which has been in use for two years, has been described by Bernard Lenelle, co-chair of the SMPG Corporate Actions Working Group as an STP-enabler, facilitating the creation and processing of events.

From an American perspective

Efforts towards faster processing in the United States have had less stimulus from needing to harmonise practices across borders. Nevertheless, significant resources have been devoted to improving processes. In the forefront of this campaign have been DTCC, the Asset Management Forum (AMF) and Industry Standardization for

---

[67] It is possible to see a version of the Event Interpretation Grid as a guest in the documents area of the SMPG website.

Institutional Trade Communication (ISITC). A DTCC subsidiary provides the Global Corporate Actions validation service, a source of 'scrubbed' corporate actions notices from around the globe made available on a subscription basis to industry participants. ActionsXchange, owned by Fidelity Investments, is another event notice subscription service, covering 1.6 million corporate actions in 2006. The Securities Industry Association (SIA) has lobbied the SEC to change the requirements for event notifications, particularly in the area of M&A.

Taking standards (and e-standards) a stage further

In essence ISO 15022 is a dictionary of approved phrases (for our purpose corporate actions phraseology), with SWIFT as the compiler, and with instructions on combining phrases (message design rules).

Logically, various different web formats (mark up languages) could be used for ISO 15022 although, as it happens, SWIFT uses just one, and that of its own devising, for its ISO 15022 messages. Other players in the corporate actions industry whose web-based applications use languages such as XML need to convert SWIFT notifications to suit.

The next stage after ISO 15022 is a new standard, **ISO 20022**, which came into being at the end of 2004. The new standard has a greater scope which covers, among other topics, notifications relating to voting at shareholder meetings. However, the fundamental change is that the standard mandates a standardised XML format. It styles itself as UNIversal Financial Information message script (UNIFI). SWIFT foresees the two standards co-existing for an unspecified length of time and has committed itself to mapping ISO 20022 messages onto the existing ISO 15022 so that no organisation's STP should suffer as a result of the change.

Corporate action systems

Investment in back office systems dived after the bursting of the dotcom bubble at the start of the decade, but was once more the focus of attention as industry participants became more aware of the risks of mistakes in corporate actions processing. Traditionally, with few benefits expected from compatibility between players, in-house development was most common. As the possibilities of automation and standardisation have become more apparent, corporate actions IT requirements have become clearer. In-house development remains significant but there are a number of major providers of corporate actions processing solutions.[68]

Corporate actions solutions vendors: the market place

Xcitek – founded in 1986 and acquired by Interactive Data in 2007, itself 62% owned by Pearson PLC – pre-eminent in North American corporate actions data delivery (and providing delivery to downstream processing systems) under the XPS

TCS (Tata Consultancy Services) – developed NCS Corporate Actions – NCS won the contract for the overhaul of DTCC's corporate actions processing legacy systems in 2005, work due to be completed in 2009

CheckFree – improved the now highly regarded (CheckFree) eVent™ solution after it acquired Heliograph in November 2003

---

[68] Celent forecast global investment of $830m on corporate actions solutions between 2003 and 2007, of which $484m would be developed by industry participants in-house. A high profile example of in-house development is Goldman Sachs where, for example, the Custody Technology team develop software solutions for the bank's private wealth management business.

GoldenSource – a leading provider in the related field of enterprise data management (EDM) – owned by Financial Technologies International, which also sells StreetActions, a corporate actions processing solution

SmartStream – majority owned by private equity fund TA from September 2006 – claims 38% of transaction lifecycle solutions for its TLM brand

Information Mosaic – founded in 1997 by John Byrne and based in Dublin – developed CAMA™, Corporate Action Management Application, judged the most advanced in 2006

Vermeg – founded in 1994 and with its HQ in Paris (and a research centre in Tunisia), Vermeg has developed Megacor, the first solution to be awarded the SWIFTReady seal of approval

Progress towards automation to date

In 2005 Pamela Brewster of Celent, the technology strategy consultancy, was quoted as saying that the majority of global custodians had achieved 70% or more automation, but only 20-25% of industry participants as a whole had achieved substantial automation.[69] The predicted path for automation was for it to take hold firstly among those, such as prime brokers and custodians, servicing third parties in the corporate actions field, while participants in private wealth mnagement and asset managers were expected to progress more slowly.

---

[69] 'Standard Action', by Rekha Menon, *Investor Services Journal*.

Measuring progress

BISS (Benchmarking International Systems and Services), based in the UK, runs the most widely acknowledged accreditation scheme for corporate actions systems and software. BISS publishes an annual report on their benchmarking findings in the corporate actions field.

SWIFTReady is a labelling scheme designed to identify solution providers who are SWIFT partners and SWIFT-compliant. CAMA, eVent, Megacor, NCS and XPS were all 'SWIFTReady' in 2007. Holders of the SWIFTReady label have to reapply each year.

The limits of standardisation

Commentators point out that issuers and, more especially, their agents are constantly evolving new classes of security with events whose exact form has not seen the light of day before. Naren Patel of CheckFree predicts that as much as 20% of corporate actions may never be automated because the asset classes they relate to never gain universal acceptance in the investment industry.[70]

One further recent development has been the marketing of the "Software as a Service" (SaaS) model of partial outsourcing by corporate actions software vendors, especially among fund managers and broker dealers. This approach allows the client fund manager or broker to delegate not only the creation of their processing system to an

---

[70] Naren Patel also worked for SWIFT on ISO 15022 implementation.

outside supplier but to tap into the supplier's expertise when it comes to fine-tuning or customising the software to their precise needs. The main challenge of SaaS is that the fund manager or broker has to be confident that data about their investments and their clients will not be misused once it moves on to the software vendor's systems.

Significant progress has been achieved in automation in the last five years, but the setbacks in the banking and investment industries in 2007 may cause a slow down in investment in improved corporate actions processing from here on.

7.

Corporate Actions Wreaking Change on Shares

How a shareholding can change even if you do not lift a finger

For an understanding into just how radical the effect of corporate actions can be, a look at one particular company over a period of three years throws up some useful insights.

Hereward Ventures came to the Alternative Investment Market (AIM) in February 2001 as a minerals exploration company with prospecting licences in Bulgaria and Ireland. In 2003, the company's strategy was switched from mineral exploration assets to hydrocarbon interests.

Take, for example, a shareholding in Hereward Ventures of 115,000 shares at the end of 2003, which would have been worth approximately £5,000; the shares trading at about 4.4p each. A year later the shares were worth about 4.8p each. Our notional shareholding would have been worth about £5,500 and represented approximately 0.00078% of the company's shares in issue.

On 17th March 2005 Hereward Ventures announced it would be holding an EGM on 11th April. Clients of an online share dealing service would have been notified about a week later and would have had until 4th April to indicate that they wished to attend the meeting or vote by proxy.[71] The EGM approved the following changes:

- Hereward's mining interests were sold to its sister company, Cambridge Minerals, for £772,000 worth of the latter's shares.

- The **consolidation** of the existing share capital of Hereward Ventures on the basis of one new ordinary share for every five existing ordinary shares.

- A **share placing** (not a rights issue) of just under 15 million new ordinary shares to raise about £3.5 million.

- The change of the company's name to Oil Quest Resources PLC.

---

[71] This assumes that one's share dealing service allows proxy votes.

Following the extraordinary meeting the number of shares in the shareholding in this example would have been reduced to 23,000 but this would now only be a 0.00052% share stake.

From late 2005 until February 2006 the shares of Oil Quest Resources were suspended as the company was in talks about a reverse takeover. The move was designed to 'gain more critical mass with the intention of developing into a significant E&P company'. Details of this deal were announced on 7th February 2006. The EGM held on 2nd March approved these changes:

- Oil Quest was to acquire the EnCore companies.

- There would be an issue of approximately 48.5 million shares 'pursuant to the acquisitions' (that is an issue of Oil Quest shares to existing EnCore shareholders). These shares would be issued at price of 15.625p, the price obtaining when the shares were suspended three months previously).

- It would change its name (again) to EnCore Oil PLC.

- Simultaneously, 112 million new shares would be issued, again at a price of 15.625p.

Reverse takeovers

A reverse takeover is one in which the control of the merged companies goes to the shareholders and management of the company that is (in legal terms) being taken over. Such mergers are usually achieved through a purchase with equity (rather than

---

cash) and they are sometimes used as a way for gaining a stock market listing.

The Oil Quest – EnCore merger exhibits all these characteristics with the shares issued to EnCore shareholders outweighing the 44.3 million shares held by existing Oil Quest shareholders. The Oil Quest directors all stepped down to be replaced by the existing directors of EnCore.

The issue of 112 million new shares did not relate directly to the merger but was to finance exploration by the merged company. The majority of this share issue was bought (privately) by investment funds such as AXA Framlington and Fidelity International.

Following these events, our imaginary shareholding would now only amount to 0.00011 per cent of the shares in issue. As the documentation pointed out this represented a 362% **dilution** of the existing Oil Quest shares. Not only was there no rights issue but none of the new shares issued were offered for sale to the public; although there was nothing to stop a shareholder buying more shares on the open market. The good news was that for a couple of months after the takeover EnCore Oil shares were trading at above or close to 30p a share, a price that would have netted our imaginary shareholder £1,900 profit had he/she decided to call it a day. Presumably the market was impressed by the interest of highly regarded investment funds in the company.

There have been two further share issues since Oil Quest became EnCore Oil; one for cash, and the second to pay the acquisition of other companies. The number of shares in issue has risen to 271 million. The shareholding in this illustration is now only 0.00008% of the issued shares.

Knowledge is power, sometimes

A company changes its name (twice), initiates an entirely new departure in its core business, not to mention massive dilutions of its shares, the wholesale changeover of its directors and even a period when trading in the shares was suspended. Although there were two EGMs called to approve changes, small investors, had they wanted to, would never have had a hope of preventing these events.

The story of Hereward/Oil Quest/EnCore could be interpreted as a lesson not to buy "penny stocks", at least not ones where the shares are closely held. It throws a spotlight on to the powerlessness of the investor with a small stake and the likelihood that those investing on their own account will be oblivious to the real story about the companies whose shares they are purchasing. Blissful ignorance is the danger that retail investors run in relation to corporate actions. The investor's only real protection is to be well informed about shares they have not yet purchased but might be about to, and to stay abreast of news about the shares they buy. The challenge of keeping informed is greater in the case of small-cap companies whose corporate actions normally receive scant attention in the press.

However, the small investor is not necessarily the victim in these circumstances. The other side of the coin is that the investor in Hereward Ventures would have done rather well out of the investment over the three year period and that, on balance, the improvement in the share price was because of these corporate actions rather than in spite of them.

An information strategy

Keeping informed on the corporate actions of companies you are investing in is not normally all-important. Even in a takeover situation, where there will be important repercussions, the investor may be well enough served by news coverage of the event rather than having to rely on specialist corporate actions information sources.

Whether investors' techniques for investment decisions rely on price charts, share tips, an understanding of particular industries and markets, share ratios or a combination of these factors, corporate actions are one further factor deserving to be taken into account in selecting and maintaining a share portfolio.

There is a wealth of information about corporate actions available on the Internet, much of it free of charge. Online corporate action information can be sourced from online share dealing services, from the websites of exchanges and issuers, and from publishers and aggregators of share information.

Information available from an issuer's 'investor relations' website

- Dividend history

- Regulatory news

- Corporate press releases

- Financial archive (including annual reports)

- Timetables for complex corporate actions

Also useful, but not always available, is information about the identity of major shareholders.

A searchable archive of the Regulatory News Service is also available on the website of the London Stock Exchange itself, and the exchange operates a free annual reports service. In some countries stock exchange announcements are only available from the exchange rather than issuers' websites. Thus, announcements about Volvo can be found by searching the company notices archive of the OMX Nordic Exchange Group.[72] Websites such as **www.ShareCrazy.com** are particularly useful for tracking recent changes to the share capitalisation of companies in the UK.

Stock exchange announcements (the Regulatory News Service)

The purpose of the Regulatory News Service (RNS) of the London Stock Exchange is to ensure that all company information that can have an effect on share prices becomes available across the investing community at the same time.

RNS includes many items that are not about corporate actions, such as announcements of trading statements or the acquisition or disposal of shares by directors. While the casual investor may be threatened with information overload, the announcements do fall into a pattern and the entire breadth of information can be grist to the investor's mill.

The LSE lost the role of exclusive publisher of RNS announcements in 2002, so there are now a number of other companies active in publishing regulatory information service material in the UK.

---

[72] www.omxgroup.com/nordicexchange.

RNS announcements should not be confused with the LSE's Corporate Events Diary, a service for brokers, asset managers and advisors that tracks what it terms 'stock situation notices' (corporate actions affecting companies quoted on the stock exchange).

For users of advisory or discretionary broking services

The ways outlined above for keeping track of corporate actions information and other corporate data are most applicable to investors who are making use of 'execution only' stockbroker services. Clients of discretionary broker services would not normally expect to be consulted when corporate events take place and advisory service clients would expect to rely on the expertise of their adviser. This begs the question of how good the experts are at identifying the client's best interests in situation such as takeovers. In time, clients of discretionary broker services may demand more evidence of their broker's expertise in taking decisions when (non-mandatory) corporate actions occur, while users of advisory services may want to be supplied with more detail and better analysis of event situations alongside the broker's advice.

Information sources for industry professionals

For professionals in the investment industry information on corporate actions should be much more readily available either directly from their provider of real-time securities price information or in the form of a feed incorporated into their real-time service from a third party. Even so, securities data providers do not tend to push their corporate actions services very hard.

Prior to their recent merger, corporate actions were an area of strength for both Thomson (Datastream) and Reuters (Datascope) but it remains to be seen how these services will be integrated.

8.

Shareholder Voting

The extent to which corporate actions are subject to shareholders' formal approval is often obscure. For example, dividend payments normally require shareholder approval but it is unusual for the voting to receive press coverage. The 'news' is what the board recommends and shareholder opposition to a board's recommendation on the dividend would be a symptom of profound shareholder unrest and lack of confidence in the management.

Events such as rights issues or returns of capital would normally be the subject of a shareholder vote. Share buyback programmes may roll on over several years after initial approval in a shareholder meeting. Shareholder votes by both acquirer and target companies are normally required for takeovers but not for the opening moves by the acquirer company. Poison pills, as an issue of shares, would normally require a shareholder vote but other strategies by takeover targets, such as **advance warning plans,** may not require a vote.

The shareholder with no teeth

Given that the shareholders are the owners of the company and that shareholder general meetings have ultimate power over the decisions the company takes, the ineffectualness of shareholder control may come as a surprise. Members of mutual organisations such as building societies are accustomed to casting votes by proxy at the society's AGM and might expect that as shareholders in a company, a similar situation would prevail.

The truth is that most small shareholders don't cast votes at shareholder meetings and that institutional investors such as investment or pension funds don't vote as often as they might.[73] The machinery is the same as

---

[73] A survey of 68 institutional shareholders by Insitutional Shareholding Services in 2006 showed that 68% of them failed to vote more than half of their stakes in foreign companies ("The Promise of E-Proxy Voting", Charles Orton Jones, Cutting edge IR, September 2007). Hugo Young of Aberdeen Asset Management is on record as observing that fund managers don't tend to turn up for AGMs in Singapore and, generally, are not interested in proxy voting. ("Proxy Voting in Singapore: Round Table Discussion", Jan. 2007).

for corporate actions but when it comes to voting it just does not work as well. One underlying reason for this weakness is that the right to vote on a specific issue at a particular shareholder meeting is an entitlement with a short shelf life in comparison to shareholders' other entitlements.[74]

The current situation is unsatisfactory in a number of ways, not least that shareholders who cannot nor will not exercise control through a company's general meetings have abdicated their responsibility for what is being done in their name. The best spur to activist shareholding is research findings that companies perform better when they have high standards of corporate governance and their (institutional) shareholders engage with them more.[75] Baldly put, shareholder voting is the stick that ensures engagement is effective and corporate governance improves.

How things have developed

Historically, institutional investors tended not to make full use of their shareholder voting rights. Typically, an insurance company or a pension fund that was unhappy with the performance of one of its investment stakes (or the behaviour of the company's management) would sell it and walk away. Such pressure as there was exerted was brought to bear behind the scenes. For some years there has been a trend towards institutional shareholders intervening more forcefully. A higher level of shareholder voting is just a part of this.

---

[74] Although, as shown in Chapter 2, corporate actions themselves can involve shareholders in choices with deadlines; for example, scrip issues normally give the shareholder the opportunity to elect to take cash instead.

[75] Research into those US companies with the highest scores for corporate governance showed that between 1991 and 1999 their shares outperformed by an average of 8.5% a year (P Gompers, J Ishii and A Metrick, "Corporate Governance and Equity Prices", *Quarterly Journal of Economics*, February 2003).

There are significant differences in the power wielded by shareholders in general meetings from one jurisdiction to the next. For instance, shareholder voting on executive pay (the board's compensation report) became mandatory in the UK in 2002. In the United States, the House of Representatives introduced the Shareholder Vote on Executive Compensation Act (sponsored by Barack Obama) in April 2007; the bill is opposed by most Republican members of Congress, and by the White House. If this becomes law it will represent an interesting intrusion of federal legislation into an area that, as mentioned in Chapter 1, has normally been regulated by the individual states.

The UK and some other European Union member states already give (larger) shareholders the right to call EGMs and add items to the agenda of a general meeting, rights that are being debated in the US but do not currently exist there. The UK's **class test provisions** uphold the right of shareholders to vote on major acquisitions and disposals, and reverse takeovers (termed Class 1 transactions). Generally, shareholder rights are stronger in the UK than the US, and UK boards of directors face a higher risk of the ultimate sanction; losing a vote in a general meeting.[76]

It is also open to issuers and third parties to attempt to win over shareholders to a proposal without calling a general meeting. In the United States it is permissible for companies to formally seek consent to changes that would normally need the approval of an extraordinary (or special) general meeting. In corporate action terms this is known as **solicitation of shareholders consent.**

In some jurisdictions a particular disincentive to voting is "share blocking". This is the practice of requiring shareholders who wish to participate in a vote to register or lodge their shares with a particular

---

[76] A lot of thought and research has gone into the subject of anti-director rights across different jurisdictions.

depository, and then denying them the freedom to trade in the shares in the lead up to the general meeting. Portugal Telecom insisted on just such a procedure for an EGM in February 2007 even though the regulator CMVM had made clear that share blocking was not a legal requirement. Greece is another country where share blocking is normal, but the European Commission is working to end the practice.

In recent times, the 2003 vote to block the severance package of Jean-Pierre Garnier at GlaxoSmithKline PLC, is probably the most celebrated instance of shareholder activism at work. However, the best sanctions are those that don't come into play too often and a high proportion of the companies with shares traded on the London Stock Exchange consult beforehand over executive compensation with the two largest shareholder trade groups, the Association of British Insurers (ABI) and the National Association of Pension Funds (NAPF).

2003 also saw an indication of the shortcomings in shareholder voting when Unilever PLC surveyed ten major shareholders who had failed to vote with all their shares at the AGM and discovered three of these institutions had issued voting instructions that the issuer never received.

'Scourge' shareholders

A host of institutional investors going through the motions of good practice in corporate governance may not be as effective as a single active investor taking the role of the leader of the opposition. Figures such as Carl Icahn in the case of Motorola, or Eric Knight in that of HSBC, may be seen as negative or even destructive, but every shareholder benefits from the spotlight they shine on the managements they harry.

Proxy Voting Agencies

These bodies, normally retained by institutional investors or fund managers, offer two main complementary services:

- Ensuring the shareholder's voting decision reaches the issuer and providing an audit trail of the process.

- Advising shareholders on voting decisions both in terms of helping them develop a voting policy and in providing research and analysis for particular voting decisions.

In the UK, two of the leading agencies are Manifest and PIRC; they also provide services relating to companies incorporated in continental Europe and the United States. Institutional Shareholder Services (ISS), part of RiskMetrics, is the leading US proxy voting agency while Proxinvest plays a leading role in France and Germany.

Shaping up

The debate about shareholder voting reached a milestone with the publication in the UK of the Myners Report in January 2004.[77] Paul Myners made the point that the shareholder voting process failed fairly often. He compared voting unfavourably with the execution of corporate actions involving a cash payment and, as Chapter 5 showed, the administration of corporate actions does not always run like clockwork. Myners placed responsibility for improving voting standards squarely in the court of the institutional investors such as

---

[77] 'Review of the impediments to voting UK shares', report by Paul Myners to the Shareholder Voting Working Group (SVWG). The SVWG was set up following the Newbold Inquiry of 1998/9, which itself worked under the aegis of the National Association of Pension Funds.

pension and investment funds (the **beneficial owners** in this case). Myners' second important recommendation was to speed up the introduction of electronic voting capabilities through Euroclear. Indeed, such was the importance he attached to this that he revisited the subject a year later. His findings were that 42% of the FTSE 100 issued share capital was voted electronically in the first half of 2005, with only two FTSE 100 companies failing to offer electronic voting.

Paul Myners' third major recommendation relates to the role of **custodians' nominees** in the model of the corporate actions process in Chapter 4. A number of custodians use a system of omnibus nominee accounts, lumping together the shareholdings of a number of beneficial owners. The effect of this practice is to slow down the identification of the stock of individual beneficial owners when a vote takes place. The report suggested that beneficial owners should consider using custodians offering share registration through a nominee with 'specific designation'. The advantages of this are akin to marking sheep to avoid confusion when different flocks become mixed up on a mountainside.[78]

The most significant development in the arena of shareholder rights since the Myners Report is the European Directive on the subject that was adopted in July 2007.[79] The purpose of the directive is to make it easier for shareholders to exercise their votes across the borders of member states. The directive covers a number of different subjects including notice periods, posting announcements of general meetings on the internet, electronic voting, the right to add items to a meeting agenda and posting voting results on issuer websites. Generally speaking, the requirements of the directive are already covered by

---

[78] Myners retained the services of the Epona consultancy for this section of his report and their findings were that a universal system of specific designation, even for just institutional investors, would probably be impracticable on grounds of cost. Myners supports specific designation for the top 200 UK pension funds and the same number of other investment vehicles.

[79] The EU Directive n° 2007/36/CE on the exercise of shareholders' rights.

existing legislation in France, Germany and the UK, though Germany does not yet allow electronic voting.

The retail investor

As mentioned at the beginning of the chapter, small investors have not commonly had an opportunity to vote in shareholder meetings. The Myners Report merely pointed out that private investors could choose a custodian that offered registration of shares in designated accounts. However, the fact of the matter is that most popular share-dealing services does not offer voting services because they are competing with one another on the basis of dealing charges and the cost of administering such a service would mean a significant increase in their overall costs. This is perfectly understandable, but they should probably make the loss of voting rights a little clearer to prospective clients.

That said, there are private client stockbrokers who have facilitated shareholder voting. For example, Brewin Dolphin has a full "Vote Your Shares" online service and Hoodless Brennan's terms and conditions commit them to contacting clients with regard to shareholder votes and corporate events in general. Other online and telephone stockbroking services will alert shareholders of an upcoming EGM but the amount of information provided may be woefully inadequate.[80] There is even less concern over involving small investors in the AGMs of the companies they invest in.

Since the Companies Act 2006 came into force the situation for retail investors holding shares through nominee accounts has changed in that the nominee can, if they choose, grant 'information rights' to the beneficial owner of the share. The information covered by this change

---

[80] For example, the Oil Quest EGM in 2006 referred to in Chapter 7 was described by one share dealing service merely as a name change, subject to shareholder approval.

are items such as the accounts and notice of general meetings (with details of possible voting rights). The default medium for the information is the nominee's website. As the grant of information rights is optional rather than mandatory it looks as if considerable variation will continue from one stockbroking service to another when it comes to voting rights.[81]

A few fine distinctions in voting terminology

A **show of hands** – gives each shareholder attending the meeting a single vote (but in a case where the chairman holds proxies which he believes would result in the opposite decision to that of the show of hands he must demand a poll).

A **poll** – gives every shareholder present in person or by proxy one vote for every share they own.

Vote withheld – Paul Myners' report called for shareholders to have the option to have recorded that they have 'withheld' their votes as an alternative to casting votes 'for' or 'against'.

Majority voting (for directors) – a hot topic in the US where plurality voting for directors is the norm, allowing some directors to be voted onto the board with very few votes. It is not uncommon for US shareholders to be given no option to cast a "no" vote and for a very few "yes" votes to swing a vote (no matter how many abstentions there are).

---

[81] The precise effect of the Companies Act 2006 in this is complex. The act also allows quoted companies to amend their articles to permit nominees (that is registered members) to nominate whoever they please to enjoy information and proxy voting rights. Presumably, this could be useful when votes came up while shares had been lent (see Chapter 12). The new voting rights for beneficial owners only apply to companies on the Official List. Generally speaking, the 2006 act seems to fall short of being a charter for proxy voting rights for all retail investors.

Where a UK retail stockbroking service offers clients the option of holding their own share certificates, they should be able to vote.[82] Likewise, **CREST** personal membership offers retail investors the opportunity of holding their securities in electronic form in their own name and many private client investment management services will act as sponsors for personal members.

Where stockbrokers offer **discretionary portfolio** services (where investment decisions are taken on your behalf), it follows that clients are not contacted by the stockbroker about voting decisions.

The one occasion when the private investor may have more, rather than less, effect than institutional shareholders on a company general meeting is if they take the trouble to turn out for the meeting in person and use the opportunity to put questions to the chair. They are entitled to do so, as long as the questions relate to the business specified in the notice of the meeting.

Just how much it matters that so many private investors do not have the opportunity to vote in shareholder meetings is a moot point. In the UK private investors holdings in the top 350 companies currently fluctuates at around 11-12% of the market's total capitalisation. This means that there are relatively few companies where private individuals as a group have shareholdings that compare with the top institutional shareholders in a company; traditionally, one exception has been Marks & Spencer and some privatisation and de-mutualisation stocks. The result is that the lost votes of private shareholders would rarely have the potential to swing votes at general meetings. The lost votes of institutional shareholders do have that potential and, moreover, failure to vote

---

[82] There are drawbacks in holding your own share certificates in terms of security and extra administrative effort.

suggests a lack of interest in the longer-term future of the companies in question.

From the point of view of the small, private investor the loss of opportunities to vote in shareholder meetings is less serious than the lack of corporate actions information, which can prevent them from making informed decisions about their investments.

Shareholder opinion in the new digital world

The IT revolution is opening up the whole subject of democratic participation in decision making in many different arenas. It is not difficult to foresee a revolution in the role and work of political leaders as a result. In the corporate world, where make or break issues are not quite as frequent (at least for individual companies), the effects of technology on investor relations are already being seen. The main result so far is an improvement in the quality and timeliness of information. Yet to become clear are areas such as the following: the degree of interest from smaller investors, how strictly the information level playing field for all shareholders will be enforced, whether shareholder votes will become more frequent, and whether shareholder opinion polling will come to play a significant role in the direction in which companies move.

9.

Corporate Actions and Taxation

Corporate actions often result in tax liabilities for investors, chiefly for Income Tax arising from dividends, or for Capital Gains Tax (CGT) arising from alterations to the investors' shareholding; for example in a takeover or a rights issue. Stamp Duties (or Stamp Duty Reserve Tax – SDRT) and withholding taxes may also result from issuers' corporate action policies. In the case of the level of Corporation Tax payable, which shareholders may view as an indirect tax on themselves, corporate actions have no impact. However, companies based in countries such as the Republic of Ireland, where corporation tax is levied at 12.5%, may have more after-tax profits with which to pay dividends.[83]

Stamp Taxes

Stamp Duty and SDRT are payable on rights issues and options to buy shares but not on scrip dividends; as an alternative form of dividend, these are liable to tax at the same level as if they were dividends.

Withholding Tax

Withholding taxes are taxes on income in respect of investments paid abroad. They apply to dividends but can also apply to interest payments, rental income or royalties. They are necessarily flat-rate as the foreign owners of the investments will not be filing tax returns in the home country of the company paying them the income. However, there can be marked differences in the level of withholding taxes levied from one country to another, and between the withholding tax levied on dividends and, for instance, that on royalties, with the latter being higher. Normally, withholding taxes will vary between 5-15% when

---

[83] Irish Corporation Tax is levied at 12.5% for 'trading' activities, 25% for investment and rental activities and just 10% for classified industrial concerns.

there is a tax treaty between the issuer's country and the shareholder's. However, some countries, such as the Netherlands, Ireland and Switzerland, levy no withholding tax at all.[84]

For citizens of the United Kingdom, to prevent double taxation and where a tax treaty is in force, tax relief is given on the lower of the following:

- The minimum foreign (withholding) tax payable under the tax treaty

- The maximum UK income tax payable

Thus a UK shareholder paying income tax on dividends at the (current) lower rate of 10% would be entitled to claim relief of 5% where a 15% withholding tax had already been charged on their dividend.

Capital Gains Tax (CGT)

Hopefully, dividends and the income tax payable on them will be fairly predictable. However, the same advantage does not apply to changes in shareholdings (initiated by corporate actions) and the CGT liabilities that arise from them. Each of the following may result in a CGT liability:

- Rights issue

- Takeover/merger (including **exchange offers**)

- Spin off/de-merger (also including **exchange offers**)

- Return of capital

---

[84] Companies can be liable for withholding taxes as well as individuals, typically when they repatriate profits from overseas subsidiaries.

In any year when a shareholder receives cash in payment for their shares there will be a CGT liability. When corporate events result in the shareholder receiving new securities there are implications for the eventual CGT bill, but the liability is delayed until the year in which the new securities are cashed in.

The first essential for accurate calculation of CGT liabilities is an accurate record of the date, volume and price of a share stake, the essential data for calculating the base cost of the shareholding. Secondly, the investor needs to keep track of all subsequent increases or decreases in that stake, whether they arose from straightforward share dealings or as a result of corporate actions.[85]

Valuing nil-paid rights

If a shareholder sells subscription rights nil-paid, it might seem that capital gain is the entire amount of the sale as the investor did not pay anything for them. However, the actual treatment of the transaction for establishing a CGT liability is based on a deemed cost of the rights, calculated as follows:

$$\frac{A \times C}{A + B} = D \text{ (the deemed 'cost' of the rights)}$$

Where,

A = the amount the nil-paid rights were sold for

B = the current value of the share stake

C = the original cost of the share stake

The capital gain would then be calculated by deducting D from A

---

[85] At the time of writing the UK government had made clear its intention to abolish taper relief in 2008, but there was some doubt that this change would be put into effect. Taper relief has been left out of consideration on the assumption that the government would follow through on its promise (or threat).

Paid-up rights

The CGT implications of paying the price of subscription rights are simple; tax will eventually be payable on the difference between the 'payment in full' price for the shares and the price obtained when selling. The shareholder merely needs to make a record of the volume and price details of this increase in their share stake.

Takeovers

A takeover offer of cash for shares will trigger an immediate CGT liability.

However, takeovers can often comprise a number of elements. For example, the takeover of Scottish Power by the Spanish company Iberdrola, in April 2007, was an offer combining cash, a special dividend (subject to income tax instead of CGT) and shares in the new parent company. In this case the shareholders were allowed to choose the proportions of the offer that they wished to take in shares in the acquiring company or in cash, making it a **mix-and-match** offer.[86]

---

[86] 'Mix-and-match' offers leave the acquiring company with the final say regarding the precise combination of cash and shares each shareholder receives. Any final offer will place fixed amounts of cash or shares on the table and individual shareholders' preferences in aggregate have to match these amounts. Typically, an issuer making a mix and match offer would state that any election under such a facility 'will only be satisfied to the extent that other shareholders make equal and opposite elections'.

The key stage for the purposes of CGT calculations (and for pinpointing the precise value of the offer) is the first day of trading after the takeover has become effective.[87] Taking an imaginary takeover offer of £5 cash plus 0.15 of a company Y share for each share in company X (the target) the calculation will look like this:

> Price of Y shares on first day of trading after the takeover becomes effective = £20
>
> Value of offer = £8 per share in company X (£5 in cash + £3 in Y's shares)
>
> A shareholding 1,000 of shares in X that had been acquired for £4,000 will now have to be apportioned by being divided in two in a ratio of 5 to 3. The base cost for calculating the CGT liability for the cash element will be £2,500 (£4,000 x 5/8ths). This element of the shareholding has now been sold to company Y for £5,000, giving a capital gain of £2,500.
>
> The base cost for calculating the future CGT liability for the element paid for in Y shares will be £1,500 (£4,000 x 3/8ths).

Had Company Y included a **mix-and-match** facility in its offer and the shareholder elected to take payment solely in Y shares (and assuming company Y had not had to scale back that election), the base cost of the shareholder's new company Y share stake would remain £4,000.

---

[87] In an instance of a takeover by a foreign company there could be two uncertainties affecting the value of the offer; firstly, the predator company's share price on that day and, secondly, the exchange rate for the currency in which the predator company's shares are traded.

The tax authorities have the last word when it comes to the share prices used to make CGT calculations. A share price at close of trading on a particular day is one method. Another, used in Australia, is to take a volume weighted average price of the shares for a specified number of trading days up to the implementation date. Sometimes, the issuer will apply to the tax authorities to confirm in advance the ratio on which the apportionment of the cost base should be made.

Loan note facilities

In the above example the shareholder is well below the threshold for paying UK CGT. Were they to have made a larger capital gain from this situation or have other capital gains to declare in the same tax year, they would welcome the option to receive **loan notes** from the acquirer in lieu of (immediate) cash. This enables the shareholder to postpone the CGT liability to later years when he will have some spare CGT allowance to use up. Loan notes normally receive interest, on which income tax will be payable.

Loan note alternatives can also be offered where a return of capital is taking place. In these instances the issuer may build a reputation for offering or failing to offer loan notes. In 2005 Royal Dutch Shell eventually caved in to shareholder complaints that its restructuring plans were exposing them to unwelcome tax liabilities by offering a loan note alternative. However, investors have no way of foretelling if the issuer will be considerate enough to issue loan notes.

Spin-offs/de-mergers

Spin-offs or de-mergers such as the divestment of Biffa by Severn Trent (see Chapter 2) have similar CGT implications to a takeover offer, including an exchange of shares.[88] Provided certain criteria are met, the shares the investor receives in the de-merged company will be treated as an **exempt distribution** and will not be liable to tax as if they were income. However, CGT will be relevant when the shares in the de-merged company come to be sold.[89]

---

[88] Appendix II shows the CGT calculation for the spin off of Biffa from Severn Trent in 2006.

[89] The Income and Corporation Taxes Act is the defining legislation in the UK.

Return of capital

A shareholder receiving a return of capital may be liable for Income Tax or CGT depending upon the manner in which the issuer handles the event.[90] For example, the issuer may divide the distribution for tax purposes into a capital element (subject to CGT) and an income element (subject to Income Tax). Normally, the issuer will ask for HM Revenue and Customs to confirm its acceptance of the approach the issuer is taking. It is common for issuers to make a return of capital that gives the shareholder a choice of receiving the sum due as income in the form of a dividend or redeemable 'B' shares that count as a capital gain. A further refinement is to offer delayed redemption of the 'B' shares so that the shareholder has some choice about the tax year in which they realise the capital gain (as with loan notes, see above).

ISAs & corporate actions

Investors who hold shares in Individual Savings Accounts (ISAs) do not escape the basic 10% dividend tax but higher rate taxpayers do avoid paying any more tax on their dividends.

ISA holders may run into complications in the event of a rights issue in that the shareholder can only elect to take up their rights if there is sufficient cash within the ISA for them to do so. This should be possible with a Maxi ISA that has a cash component as well as a share component, but you cannot import cash into an ISA just to pay for the rights call. Sometimes an ISA holder may sell some of the rights nil-paid in order to have sufficient funds to pay for the remainder.

---

[90] The tax treatment of events such as return of capital varies from one jurisdiction to another. For example, some countries (such as Canada) have 'capital dividends' while in the US, the term 'return of capital dividend' is used.

An investor with a Mini share ISA (with no cash component) would have to pass up the opportunity to acquire more shares in a rights issue unless there was sum cash awaiting investment. However, interest on cash waiting to be invested is taxed at 20% and the ISA provider may not pay a good rate of interest on this cash in any case.

It is not unknown for ISA providers to prevent investors from benefitting from events such as rights issues, so investors would be well advised to read the terms and conditions of their ISA provider to make sure there are no surprises when these situations arise.[91]

The tax effects of corporate actions for holders of investment funds

Although investment funds are on the receiving end of corporate actions as entitlements arising from the investments they hold, the only events that they originate are the interest or dividends paid by the fund. Interest or dividends paid by UK authorised investment funds (AIFs) are taxable in the same way as they would be on any other investment.[92]

The investor will have a capital gains calculation to make when they come to sell their investment in a unit trust or OEIC but the investment fund itself does not face a CGT charge from realising capital gains from its individual investments.

---

[91] From April 2008 the ISA regulations change to allow holders of cash ISAs to move them into shares, but this may not help an investor needing some tax sheltered cash to pay for rights in full. It looks as if, in order to take advantage of this change, the whole of a cash ISA would have to be converted into equities, which may be more cash than is needed for the rights.

[92] Investors in funds who have opted for accumulation units have to pay income tax as if they had received the income rather than using it to purchase the extra units.

The tax situation for US investors in mutual funds is quite different. American mutual funds are required to make an annual pay-out of any net realised capital gains to fund shareholders (a **capital gains distribution**).[93] The taxable gain depends on the length of time that the fund has been invested in the stock, not on the period of time that the shareholder has been invested in the fund. The unwary investor could find themselves in the position of seeing the value of their own investment in a fund show a loss but still facing a tax bill for the 'capital gain distribution' arising from the previous year.

---

[93] These realised capital gains will arise from investment initiatives by the fund itself but could also arise from corporate actions such as a cash takeover bid.

10.

Corporate Actions in Other Jurisdictions

Different laws, different taxation systems and different customs combine to ensure that, although corporate actions are a global industry, there are innumerable surprises facing an investor venturing into foreign markets. There is no grand theory to explain all the differences that exist between different jurisdictions, and the ones spotlighted here do not comprise an exhaustive list. Rather they are simply intended as a caution against making unwarranted assumptions on the basis of knowledge of one's home market.

Japanese dividends

Japanese practice for the payment of dividends is a good example of just how markedly different a foreign jurisdiction can be. Japan differs from the typical European or American model by having no ex-dividend date. Instead the year-end, universally the end of December, is the record date for establishing eligibility for a dividend. However, no one knows for sure how big the dividend will be until after it has been approved by the company AGM, which almost always takes place at the end of the following June.

Dividends from emerging markets

In the case of emerging economies the delay in receiving dividends can be a significant factor for institutions. Quite often investors can wait two or three months after the ex-date for a dividend to be paid. This means a considerable loss of potential interest on the dividend.[94]

Depository receipts

These are a convenience to help investors avail themselves of overseas investment opportunities through their domestic stock market. The practice began in the United States and depository receipts that can be traded on US exchanges are called American Depository Receipts (ADRs). However, depository receipts may also be tradable globally (Global Depository Receipts – GDRs) or be sold in other specific regions such as the European Union (EDRs) or Australia, where they are known as CHESS Depositary Interests (CDIs), CHESS being the Australian electronic share trade clearing system.

---

[94] 'Corporate Action Processing, What are the Risks?' (Oxera, 2004).

Depository receipts will normally bundle small numbers of ordinary shares in a company. Normally they are sold by (custodian) banks and they can be sponsored, by the issuer of the shares, or unsponsored, in which case the bank's stockbroking division will have initiated the process.

Typically, holders of ADRs should enjoy eligibility for all corporate actions and elections, and should be entitled to proxy votes at shareholder meetings. In addition they benefit from receiving all cash benefits in their own currency, which can simplify tax returns.

An additional benefit for investors is that, where the issuer's country of origin has weak investor protection, they enjoy a measure of protection from the investor's domestic regulatory authority.[95]

Restrictions on share ownership

Restrictions on foreign ownership may arise from national or supranational laws or the company's own rules. Switzerland and the Nordic countries have such restrictions as do several of the emerging markets. Restrictions on the ownership of shares in companies that are important to national defence and security are also widespread.

In recent years the controversy in the USA over the takeover of P&O by Dubai Ports World is the most high profile instance of restrictions on

---

[95] Several jurisdictions place restrictions on the sale of foreign securities. In the US the law prohibits the selling of securities except through national (ie, US) securities exchanges. This is the reason why a UK rights issue prospectus, for example, will begin with a list of jurisdictions where the prospectus is not for publication or distribution. Depository receipts are a sensible and perfectly legal way of sidestepping these issues.

foreign ownership affecting a corporate event situation. This episode was unusual in that Congress only intervened once the takeover bid was well underway. Normally, the legal restriction on the foreign ownership of shares is already in place and the implications for corporate actions, though latent, are made clear by the issuer.

For example, in the European Union there is a requirement for air carriers to be owned and effectively controlled by EU nationals.[96] As a result the articles of association of companies, such as Ryanair, include stipulations designed to prevent majority control of the company passing into the hands of non-EU member state citizens. The articles in the case of Ryanair go as far as permitting a compulsory sale of particular shareholders' holdings to EU nationals and preventing non-EU nationals from attending general meetings or voting.[97] The company maintains a **Separate Register** of "affected shares" in order to be able to identify the non-EU shareholders and carry out these radical corporate actions.

For a company whose foreign shareholdings are repeatedly approaching or passing the upper limit there is the possibility of a dual market developing which could be advantageous for domestic shareholders.

Variations in rules for general meetings

The practice of requiring two-thirds majorities for some resolutions to be passed at general meetings is fairly widespread. For example, Swiss company law requires a two-thirds majority vote for, among other things, the introduction of voting shares, conditional and authorised capital increases, and restrictions or exclusion of shareholders' pre-emptive rights.

---

[96] European Union Regulation 2407/92.

[97] Ryanair Holdings PLC, SEC Form 20-F, 27th September 2006 (the Annual Report).

Different countries have variations in the treatment of ordinary shares and preference shares when it comes to voting. Some jurisdictions, such as Mexico, allow for a class of 'restricted voting shares', which give preference shareholders a vote on resolutions for the dissolution of a company, mergers or spin-offs.[98]

Some countries provide for specific board representation of minority shareholders. In Brazil, holders of preference shares with a certain combined shareholding have a right to elect one director, as do holders of common stock.[99]

The treatment of minority shareholders is one of the most important considerations for investors in emerging markets, second only to the volatility of the markets themselves. While private foreign investors are unlikely to be entering the Chinese or Indian markets in large numbers individually for a few years, emerging market investment funds will be watching the regulators' approach to corporate actions. This includes monitoring mergers and divestments as well as the quality of shareholding information that is made available.

Beneficial owners of shares

Japanese company law does not recognise voting rights for the beneficial owners of shares. However, there is a national proxy voting platform and the commercial code does allow the registered shareholders (normally trust banks) to abdicate their voting powers (to the platform) as a means of passing voting rights back to the beneficial owners. As in the UK, technology is permitting greater participation by (beneficial) shareholders.

---

[98] 'Corporate Governance in the Major Economies of the Americas', Morgan Lewis, 2004.

[99] There are big variations in minority shareholders' rights to elect directors across jurisdictions. Some allow what is known as 'cumulative voting' whereby shareholders abdicate their right to vote for all the board changes due at a general meeting, but in exchange may 'concentrate' their votes on a single director of their choice. Cumulative voting is allowed in Canada and the United States.

While proxy voting rights are well established in the United States, historically stockbrokers have been permitted to vote on a broad range of routine issues without referring back to the beneficial owners of the stock. With effect from 2008 the New York Stock Exchange has changed its rules so that the appointment of directors of a quoted company ceases to be one of these routine matters.

Over-voting problems on Wall Street

In June 2006 New York Stock Exchange Regulation Inc. fined some of Wall Street's most prestigious investment banks for poor supervision of the proxy votes. Although the banks normally delegate the work of contacting beneficial share owners to proxy service agents, they were still liable for discrepancies identified by tabulators between the numbers of shares voted and the information on shareholdings at record date held by the DTCC. Similar problems have been identified in Canada and the European Union.

Bearer certificates

In fact, bearer share certificates are very common indeed, just not normally found in the case of large quoted companies. They are a common form of certification for self-employed people in the United Kingdom who buy an off-the-shelf company to trade under. The 2006 Companies Act continued to allow bearer certificates for UK companies even though they can be used to disguise the ownership of companies and to shelter resources that would otherwise be taxable. Bearer share certificates instead of share registers still prevailed in Nevada and

Wyoming in the USA until anti-terrorism legislation was used to compel an end to the practice. Tax havens such as the British Virgin Islands have recently taken steps to make it compulsory for bearer share certificates to be lodged with a custodian bank. Bearer certificates are also widespread among German companies and are a complicating factor in arranging shareholder meetings.

Bearer share certificates – use and misuse

Enjoying the benefit of corporate actions from an issuer when share certificates are in bearer form may present problems where there are more than a handful of shareholders; how does the issuer know whom to pay the benefit to? Normally, such companies will be closely held but that is not to say that publicly quoted companies might not be caught up in the activities of offshore companies with bearer share certificates.

In 2005 Walt Anderson, the founder of Telco Communications and Esprit Telecom, was indicted in a US Federal District Court for tax evasion. He had used British Virgin Islands companies to transfer ownership of his holdings of stock in Telco and Espirit in the 1990s. This was achieved before public offerings in the stock of Telco and Esprit and before substantial rises in the value of these stocks. The ultimate ownership of the transferred stock was anonymous; the holding company, Iceberg, had bearer share certificates. These were eventually discovered in Mr Anderson's home and the location was sufficient proof that Mr Anderson was the owner.[100]

---

[100] Walt Anderson's tax affairs were covered in detail by David Hilzenrath in the *Washington Post* in April 2005.

In the realm of fixed interest securities (which will be the focus of the next chapter) bearer bonds have a less shady reputation than bearer share certificates. The reason being that there would be no point in holding the bond if it were not for the coupon (the fixed interest payable) and to obtain the income you have to hold up your hand.

Harmonisation of corporate actions in the European Union

Mention has already been made of the part played by the European Union's Giovannini Group in efforts to standardise corporate actions.[101] In April 2007 the European Credit Sector Associations (ECSA) and the European Central Securities Depositories Association (ECSDA) reported on progress in harmonising corporate actions in the EU. The differences that have required ironing out chiefly relate to different dating arrangements for corporate actions and enhancements to the supply of information by issuers to central securities depositories and on to investors. Some countries, such as Italy, have corporate action processing practices that work without a record date while others, such as Denmark, have a record date but positions are struck at a different time from the end of the day.

Harmonisation will require all issuers to provide translations into English of all announcements that do not conform to ISO 15022/20022 standards and corporate website summaries of corporate actions in English. The end of 2008 should see the implementation of the bulk of these harmonisation measures.[102]

---

[101] See Chapter 6. Giovannini barrier 3 is the shorthand term for the historical variations in the treatment of corporate actions between different EU member states.

[102] 'Harmonisation of Corporate Actions in Europe: Giovannini Barrier 3', 30th April 2007.

Sharia-compliant assets and corporate actions

Although not always holding sway as a fully-fledged jurisdiction, Islamic banking principles are increasingly a force to be reckoned with in the investment world. Corporate actions are one of the chief distinguishing characteristics of Sharia-compliant instruments.

Conventional interest bearing debt securities are not permitted and some high risk forms of investment are disallowed on the grounds that they too closely resemble gambling.[103]

The key requirement of Islamic finance is that investments should entail some form of profit (and risk) sharing. The main form of finance is *Mudarabah* (equity finance) which gives the investor a contract stipulating a share of a project's revenues. *Sukuk* (financial certificate) works on the same principle but normally applies to lending for property investment with leasing revenues earmarked for distribution to the investors.[104] In addition to corporate actions relating to payment and redemption, Sharia-compliant instruments will normally need to allow for early redemption (or settlement) in the event that the issuer is unable to continue ensuring the Sharia-compliant status of the investment.

The Dubai International Financial Exchange provides depository services for (some) Sharia-compliant assets. A number of global custodians provide a custody service for these assets.

---

[103] For example, shorting, day trading, futures and options. Sharia does not permit taking positions in securities without actually owning them.

[104] Islamic financing includes a range of instruments covering deferred payment arrangements, debt financing, leasing and lease to purchase.

The current situation in China

While corporate actions in mainland China are not exceptional, the structure of the country's stock market has been so different from that of other nations that the process of transformation needs to progress further before clear comparisons with corporate actions in other parts of the world can be made. From the point of view of overseas investors the biggest contrast is the restriction of inward investment in stocks to Qualified Foreign Institutional Investors.[105] These will normally have been assisted in applying to trade on the Chinese market by a QFll custodian, such as Citigroup Global Transaction Services. The QFll custodian acts as a link between the QFlls and the China Securities Regulatory Commission as well as channelling corporate action information and payments from Chinese issuers.

Looming far larger in terms of the impact on corporate actions is the ongoing transformation of the split capital share structure of many Chinese companies. Until April 2005 the normal pattern of ownership for Chinese companies was split between publicly tradable stock and non-tradable state-owned shares in a proportion of 1 to 2. The state share reform initiated by the China Securities Regulatory Commission at that date requires an end to what was known as the 'segregated equity ownership' regime.[106] Achieving this revolution required a wave of (once only) corporate actions as the hither-to non-tradable state-owned equity was transformed into tradable stock.

---

[105] The QFll regime dates from 2002. There is also a category of foreign investor known as 'strategic investors'; these will normally be entities such as private equity firms investing (and sometimes acquiring complete ownership) on their own behalf rather than retail investment funds.

[106] Not to be confused with the distinction between A shares, which are listed in Shanghai and Shenzhen, and H shares, listed in Hong Kong.

The precise details of the process varied from one corporation to another but it generally involved gaining the agreement of the holders of existing tradable shares to the flood of new shares that threatened to devalue their investments. Holders of the existing tradable shares were in effect bought off with offers of scrip issues, warrants or special dividends.[107] It was recognised that this process would create over-supply. Chinese sources claimed that the bulk of the transformation in share structure of Chinese corporations took place within 12 months of the policy's introduction and (luckily) this period was marked by a surge in the confidence of Chinese equity investors.[108] It may still be too early to decide if the Chinese stock market has truly digested this enormous increase in quoted stock. In the longer term the abolition of the non-tradable state-owned shares obviously opens up the way for mergers and acquisitions.

---

[107] See 'China's Capital markets at the Birth of a New Era' (Araceli Almazan & Chris Huishan Lin, UC Davis School of Law, May 2006).

[108] The enormous scale of this undertaking doesn't seem to have had the recognition it deserves overseas. The overall market capitalisation of quoted companies in mainland China in the first half of 2005 was in the region of US$125 billion. The value of the non-tradable state shares in these companies was put at US$300 billiion. A year later, when about 80% of these companies had abolished their dual share structures, some US$37.5 billion had passed to the holders of the existing tradable shares in the form of bonus shares, warrants or special cash dividends. In aggregate this is presumably the biggest corporate action in history.

11.

Corporate Actions for Debt Securities

Debt corporate actions, the most numerous in the corporate actions universe

For the UK investor, the importance of debt securities is considerably less relative to the equity market than in other developed economies. UK total non-government debt securities in issue were $825 billion in 2004 compared with $13 trillion and $1.9 trillion for the US and Japan respectively.[109] Corporate bonds are less popular than in the other countries and Treasury Rules have prevented local authorities from issuing bonds in their own name. By contrast, in the United States, the market in municipal bonds is worth $2 trillion.[110] Worldwide there are upwards of 3 million corporate actions each year relating to scheduled payments of interest and scheduled maturities for debt instruments.[111]

Recent years have seen an increase in the importance of bonds in the UK as pension and endowment funds moved to improve their solvency after the end of the dotcom bubble. The UK is also very important in the issuing of international bonds.

Debt securities are a different kind of animal from equity with different corporate events to match. However, the processing of debt securities' corporate actions is carried on by the same financial institutions in the same way that obtains for the corporate actions of shares.

---

[109] Bank for International Settlements Quarterly Review, March 2005.

[110] Reuters, 17th January 2007.

[111] 'Corporate Action Processing, What are the Risks?' (Oxera, 2004). This study gives a figure of 3 million for fixed-rate interest payments and maturities in passing. The use of the term "fixed interest" (or "fixed-income") to encompass all interest bearing securities is not strictly accurate; floating rate notes are debt securities with varying interest payments. Exact statistics on equity and non-equity corporate actions are hard to obtain as most leading players in the corporate actions industry do not distinguish between equity and debt corporate events.

The legal framework

In the UK and the rest of the European Union bond issues must comply with the EU Prospectus Directive of 2003, which was incorporated into UK law in 2005 by means of amendments to the Financial Services & Markets Act 2000. The requirements are set out in the 'Prospectus Rules' and the FSA is the regulator for the issue of new bonds and the conditions under which they may be marketed.

In the United States **bond indentures** must be registered with the Securities & Exchange Commission. Many of these indenture documents date back decades as it is not unusual for the indentures to be **open-ended,** meaning that the issuing company can issue more bonds without publishing a new bond indenture. However, the SEC would not normally allow the face value of bonds in issue to exceed the company's fixed assets.

The fundamental difference with equity corporate actions

Whether investing in **corporate** or **municipal bonds, fixed interest securities, floating rate notes** or **mortgage backed securities,** there is a fundamental difference in the status of shareholders and holders of debt securities. Whereas equity brings co-ownership of the company, debt securities such as corporate bonds are just that – debt. The citizenship analogy used in Chapter 1 does not apply to holders of debt securities. Instead the entire life of the investment is mapped out from the start in the **bond indenture,** in essence a contract between the issuer and the investor.[112]

---

[112] In the UK (and the EU as a whole) the term "prospectus" is commonly used as in the "EU Prospectus Directive'" (2003/71/EC) but this applies to both bond and share prospectuses.

This is not to say that the corporate actions of bonds and other debt securities are entirely predictable but it does mean that every corporate action contingency is spelled out in the bond indenture, making them weighty documents. It will certainly cover the level of interest, the maturity date and detail any rights on the issuer's part to make early redemption of the bond.

Interest and redemption – the main events of debt instruments

With none of the possibilities that a share in a company brings, such as rights issues or takeover bids, the range of corporate actions for the holders of debt instruments is pared down to just three: interest payments (alternatively known as coupon payments), redemption of the debt security or combinations of the two.

The bond indenture may have **call or prepayment provisions** setting terms for "in whole" or **partial redemption** of a bond. In the case of a partial redemption, the investor will continue to hold the issuer's bonds but the total interest received will be reduced. It is common (but not universal) for early redemption clauses to stipulate the redemption must coincide with an interest payment date for the bond in question.

Redemption by 'drawing'

An alternative to partial redemption or call under terms set out in the indenture is to draw bonds that are to be redeemed ahead of the final maturity date by lottery. The bond holder would know in advance when the early redemptions were due to take place but not what proportion of their holding would be redeemed at each date.

Early redemptions may be optional or mandatory. The circumstances in which a mandatory early redemption could be triggered might include the issuer's breach of either a **gearing ratio covenant,** which limits an issuer's borrowings in the lifetime of the bond, or a **negative pledge,** an issuer's undertaking not to pledge greater security of collateral to other lenders.

Depending on the terms of the bond indenture, optional early redemption can be initiated by the issuer (**callable bonds**) or the investor (**puttable bonds**). Typically, an issuer might initiate an early bond redemption voluntarily when interest rates are falling and cash can be raised more cheaply by a new bond issue or bank loans. Normally, callable bonds will have a period of **call protection** at the start of their life when the issuer is not able to exercise their right to redeem them. For the investor, 'callability' can nullify the advantage of fixed-interest, making the bonds like the hedgehogs in the game of croquet in 'Alice's Adventures in Wonderland'; unrolling themselves and walking off at the critical moment. Callable bonds are normally priced at a discount to non-callable bonds to compensate for this disadvantage. In the case of puttable bonds, the exercise of the right to 'put' the bond back to the issuer is normally restricted, under the terms of the indenture, to a specific date or dates.

Some bonds allow for more specific variations in the redemption date. It is possible for bonds to be issued with an **acceleration covenant** where occurrences such as a default or a credit rating downgrade can precipitate an early redemption. Conversely, an **extendable bond** allows the issuer to postpone redemption (though, as with callable bonds, the purchaser would normally expect a discount on this variant).

Interest payments

Within the corporate actions industry, payments of interest are lumped together with dividend payments to holders of equity under the term "income events". As with dividend payments, ownership of the security on the record date is all important when it comes to the payment of interest on debt securities. However, unlike share dividends, the price of fixed-interest bonds will always reflect the **accrued interest** in an entirely predictable way. Other things being equal, the closer in time to the **coupon date** that a trade in a fixed-interest security occurs the higher the price will be.[113] This is the so-called **dirty price** of a bond, including the accrued interest, calculated as follows:[114]

$$\textbf{Coupon} \ \ X \ \ \textbf{days from the previous coupon date to the (trade)} \\ \textbf{settlement date}$$

$$\textbf{days in the coupon period}$$

So, in corporate action terms dividend payments and interest (or coupon) payments work in a very similar way, but there is a significant difference between a share being "ex-dividend" and a bond being "ex-coupon".[115] Future interest payments on an ex-coupon bond can be precisely factored into the price the bond trades. However, when it comes to share prices, the value of future dividends payable on a share that has recently gone ex-dividend tend to be obscured by other factors[116]

---

[113] Ie, ignoring factors such as changes in interest rates generally, downgrades or upgrades by bond rating agencies, or downturns/upturns in business confidence.

[114] Bond prices quoted in the press are 'clean prices', stripped of the accrued interest that the seller will expect to receive when the trade is settled.

[115] Confusingly, sometimes bonds are referred to as being "ex-dividend".

[116] That said, there will normally be a drop in the share price of a company at the ex-dividend date if the dividend is significant.

> ## Corporate actions and debt security liquidity
>
> In the case of equity, corporate events (and financial statements) by the issuer tend to be the times of greatest trading activity, and hence liquidity. However, in the case of corporate bonds the predictability of the issuer's corporate actions means that new issues often generate a brief initial period of high trading activity levels followed by long periods with scarcely any trading at all.

Variable coupon bonds and floating rate notes

Typically, **floating rate notes** (FRNs) will offer an interest rate that is set at a pre-determined level above a particular money market rate such as LIBOR. The interest on an FRN can be reset daily, weekly, monthly, quarterly, semi-annually or annually; quarterly or semi-annual **reset dates** are the most common. Because of the link to money market rates, FRNs tend to trade at close to their par value. Those with less frequent reset dates have the potential to miss out on an interest rate spike.

Variants on the FRN include the **drop-lock FRN**, which converts itself into a fixed-rate bond when short term interest rates fall to a particular level, **capped FRNs**, where a ceiling is set for the interest rate payable, or the **mini-max FRN**, which allows for fluctuation in the interest rate between a lower as well as an upper limit.

Step-up bonds pay one rate of interest for an initial period and a specified higher rate of interest from a specified later date.

Conversions & Warrants

In addition to interest payment and redemption, the staple corporate actions of debt instruments, many of these securities are issued with metamorphic properties so that in due course they become a different type of debt instrument or a company's ordinary shares. These conversion events add a further category of corporate actions to those already mentioned.

Normally, the convertibility of the security will be made absolutely clear to the investor by the inclusion of the word "convertible" in the name (as with 'GMA Resources PLC unsecured convertible 10% loan stock 2009'). The percentage refers to the interest payable and 2009 is the year in which the loan is due for repayment if conversion has not taken place. Conversions can be mandatory or optional but the conversion ratio will normally be known at the time of issue.[117] From the investor's point of view mandatory convertible bonds or loan stock are riskier investments and normally carry a higher yield in order to compensate for this. Convertible loan stock is normally tradable with a price that reflects fluctuations in the price of the issuer's ordinary shares. If the issuer is subject to a takeover bid, a complex corporate event situation arises for the holder of convertible bonds or loan stock.[118] Often the acquiring company will offer its own convertible securities in exchange for those of the target company.[119]

---

[117] So a conversion ratio of 10 implies that the convertible security can be converted into 10 of the issuer's shares. Together with the face value of the debt security it is then possible to calculate the conversion price the issuer is offering you for the shares. An example of a debt security without a conversion rate fixed from the outset was the well publicised Abu Dhabi Investment Authority purchase of securities of Citigroup in November 2007.

[118] The ramifications for holders of convertible securities are covered in detail by The Takeover Code.

[119] Issues of convertible loan stock will bring the existing shareholders pre-emption rights into play (see. Chapter 2).

Convertibles to the rescue!

The use of convertible debt securities came to the fore with the sovereign wealth funds that came to the aid of banks such as Citigroup and Merrill Lynch after the huge losses arising from the sub-prime crisis in 2007.

Securities issued by the banks to the Abu Dhabi Investment Authority and the Korean Investment Corporation not only offered a generous coupon (9% and 11% respectively) but big discounts on the value they placed on the banks' share prices when they convert in 2009-10.

The Government of Singapore Investment Corporation (SIC) went one better with the convertible preferred securities it purchased in Citigroup in January 2008. Although the coupon on these securities is slightly lower at 7%, they come with an option to convert at a 20% discount but no fixed conversion date.

A refinement on convertible loan stock that is occasionally used is for the issuing company to make the convertible stock 'partly paid' with the investor committing to paying a second instalment of cash if and when a certain stipulated condition is satisfied. The number of shares the investor receives at conversion will depend on whether both instalments of cash were paid up for the convertible loan stock or only the first.

Warrants are instruments that give the holder an optional right to a company's shares at a future date. Warrants are not necessarily issued by the company in question; banks can also issue them and when they do so the warrants can either be **covered** or **naked**. This depends upon whether or not the issuing bank has holdings of the underlying shares to match the purchaser's entitlement when the holder chooses to exercise the warrant.[120] Companies sometimes issue bonds with warrants on their own shares in order to make the bonds a more attractive investment. Normally, these warrants are **detachable** and can be traded independently.

Investor actions can be corporate actions, too

'Putting' a bond back to the issuer for redemption, opting for the conversion of loan stock in to common stock, exercising a warrant or detaching a warrant from a bond are all instances of actions that are initiated by the investor rather than by the issuer. As such they do not fully satisfy the definition of a corporate action. Nevertheless, the processes involved in actioning these investor decisions use the same systems and technology as corporate actions in the purest sense.

Most complex of all

A further category of debt security is that of **asset backed securities**. These are debt instruments that make use of a pool of assets to provide the income stream promised to the purchaser. The way in which the interest due on these instruments (which include the now notorious mortgage-backed securities) works in corporate action terms is one of the areas of complexity that Chapter 12 will tackle.

---

[120] Not to be confused with covered bonds.

Equity and debt – make the connection

Although the corporate action entitlements of shareholders and bondholders are totally distinct, there is a sense in which the two species of security impinge upon one another. For example, a corporate bond issue could make it less likely that the same company will be turning to its equity holders for a rights issue.[121] The holders of the two kinds of security may be eating in different rooms but they are taking slices of the same turkey; it makes sense to pay attention to one another. Commentators in the press will occasionally refer to a decoupling between expectations or sentiment in the debt markets and the equity markets if, for instance, poor credit ratings do not seem to be translating into lower share prices.

The credit rating agencies will normally try to anticipate likely corporate actions for the issuer's equity and other debt securities when making their assessments on a new bond issue. Conversely, an equity issuer contemplating a new corporate action may commission a credit rating agency assessment of the impact of the action on the credit rating of its corporate bonds.

---

[121] At the time of writing, a similar effect was seen when Cadbury Schweppes announced that it was not going to pay a special dividend. The board argued that the payment of a special dividend would only be affordable if the newly de-merged Dr Pepper Snapple issued junk bonds, and problems in the debt markets made this option prohibitively expensive ('Cadbury rules out cash return', *Financial Times*, 20th February 2008).

12.

Corporate Action Effects Across the Investing Spectrum

Thishis chapter will look at the impact of corporate actions across a number of areas, including some of the more complex kinds of investing. No matter how sophisticated investments become, corporate actions will always have to follow.

Stock exchange indices

Many corporate actions can have an affect on the value and constituents of an exchange index such as the FTSE 100 or the S&P 500. The major categories of event that do not have any direct impact are capitalisation issues or consolidations and, in the case of the FTSE 100, the cash dividend.[122] The publisher of an index will normally set out the methodology for calculating a stock exchange index and this should include a detailed description of how all the main corporate actions will be handled.

The effect of a single corporate action on an index is applied by a recalculation of the **divisor** for the index in question. Normally, the index publisher will need to make multiple changes every trading day. This work is highly labour intensive and the indices publishers simplify the task using such means as only making complete recalculations on a quarterly basis.[123]

---

[122] The S&P 500 does make an adjustment to the divisor to offset the "gap down" that occurs when stock goes ex-dividend. Also, cash dividends are important when it comes to making "total return" calculations about relative benefits of investing in different classes of investment or tracking different indices.

[123] Standard & Poor's only makes same-day recalculations for the issue of new shares in cases where the new issue amounts to 5% or more of the previous number of shares in issue.

Index calculations and divisors

The divisor is the key to the chief benefit of stock exchange indices; namely, providing a comparison over time. The essential characteristics of a divisor are to have a fixed value at its fixed start date and for it to be recalculated every time a change occurs to the number of shares in issue for a constituent company.

The basic calculation for a market or cap weighted index like the FTSE 100 is as follows:

$$\frac{\textbf{Total Market Value of Index Constituents}}{\textbf{Current Divisor}^{124}} = \textbf{Index Value}$$

Corporate actions in stock charts

In order to serve their purpose of providing useful comparisons over a period of time, stock charts also require adjustments to allow for corporate actions. The process of adjusting charts is known as **re-chaining**. Re-chaining calculations have to be applied in the case of all changes to the share price that are under the direct control of an issuer, such as capitalisation (bonus) issues or consolidations. Basically, re-chaining involves adjusting the chart's historical data to show what the share price would have been if the new level of shares in issue had prevailed since the beginning of the chart period.

---

124 The trick in understanding divisors is to remember that the purpose of the index is to help the investor track changes in market capitalisation that can be ascribed to secondary market trading. The job of the divisor is to remove the distorting effect of changes to market capitalisation arising from other causes, notably corporate actions. Among the methodologies of the various indices, 'The FTSE Guide to UK Calculation Methods' is particularly helpful. The corporate actions that normally require an adjustment are as follows: rights issues, special dividends (that produce a drop in the share price), takeovers and de-mergers where the spun off company does not qualify to be included in the index. Share repurchases will also result in an adjustment.

There are some corporate actions, such as reverse takeovers, which would seem to represent such a fundamental change to the company in question that re-chaining the chart will serve no useful purpose. Charts for companies such as these should be read in tandem with the share history of the company.[125] Should a corporation decide to change its Tradable Instrument Display Mnemonic (TIDM) code after a complex event, the chart will be commenced afresh.[126]

Corporation actions and options, futures, contracts for difference and exchange traded funds

For **options** and **futures** contracts the investor should consult the exchange's methodology to check the effect on the instrument in question.[127] Bonus issues, consolidations, rights issues, special dividends, mergers and takeovers and de-mergers may all lead to adjustments but none is normally made for ordinary dividends or scrip dividends.[128] Contracts on shares that are de-listed owing to bankruptcy or liquidation receive no special treatment but a contract on a share in which trading is suspended may be allowed to continue trading. As would be expected, share repurchases on the open market tend not to be adjusted for, but where the issuer takes steps to give all shareholders equal opportunity to sell back their shares an adjustment would probably be made.

---

[125] Five or three year charts for Encore Oil, for example (cf, Chapter 7), will be useful only to an investor who bought Oil Quest shares before the reverse takeover by Encore.

[126] Formerly known as EPIC (Exchange Price Input Computer) codes. TIDMs are the equivalent of ticker symbols for US stocks.

[127] See, for example, 'Liffe's Harmonised Corporate Actions Policy'.

[128] Futures contract pricing discounts ordinary dividends; the expected dividend is built-in to the price.

Spread bets are also adjusted for most corporate actions, but not for ordinary dividends, which are built into the cost of the bet.

For (equity related) **contracts for difference** (CFDs), an adjustment for dividends is normally made with the equivalent of the dividend being credited to long positions and debited from short ones. Typically, the dividend credit will be made on the ex-dividend date rather than on the payment date. It is normal for CFD positions to be adjusted to reflect any corporate action or, alternatively, for the provider to credit or debit the client's cash account by an equivalent amount. However, investors may find variations in the extent to which they are given a choice when it comes to voluntary corporate actions or mandatory corporate actions with options. For example, some CFD providers may make it possible for holders of long positions to make an election over a voluntary event while holders of short positions are merely assigned a position that complements the elections of the holders of long positions.

As tracking investments, **exchange traded funds** (ETFs) will normally reflect all corporate actions in step with the underlying index, although the index will often make the necessary adjustment at the same time as one of its periodic rebalancing exercises rather than instantly.[129]

Corporate actions for asset backed securities

Unlike the instances above where the effects of corporate actions are achieved at one remove, **structured securities** such as collateralised debt obligations (CDOs) come with their own direct corporate action entitlements. As with other debt securities, there are only two main

---

[129] This applies to cap-weighted index ETFs and fundamental ETFs. Although Quant ETFs might be seen as a law unto themselves in terms of their selection criteria, the application of corporate actions to the fund should be straightforward. There are unlikely to be any Quant ETFs which measure actions in the process of selecting the stocks. How corporate actions will be applied to the new actively-managed ETFs remains to be seen.

corporate actions; interest payments and principal repayments. However, the manner in which interest payments and repayment of principal coincide and the frequency of events (normally monthly) make the corporate action processing for these instruments a complex affair.

The way in which structured securities and their payments (normally referred to as the "rate") operate is at variance from the processes outlined in Chapter 4. They are characterised by the very "arms-length" relationship that the issuer has with borrowers and the investors (holders). The first step is to create a **special purpose vehicle** (SPV) as a discrete entity for holding the assets (mortgages, credit card loans or hire purchase agreements) "off balance sheet" and selling the corresponding debt securities. Instead of a registrar, structured securities have a **paying agent** who issues the security's certificates to investors and provides payment information to holders of the security. Custodians in the context of structured securities are the trustees who look after mortgage documents (and other "proofs" of the underlying assets). The custodian will also have responsibility for monitoring the collection of cash and information reports about the performance of the assets.

When it comes to the payment events, the collection of interest and principal is carried out by **servicers** and **master servicers**. Servicers also handle delinquencies and defaults. Interest and principal payments then pass to the paying agent and thence to the **Depository Trust Company**. From there the payments are passed to brokers and custodians and onto the beneficial owners of the securities.

The amount of monthly payments on structured securities rose more than fivefold from 2001 to 2005.[130] Key features of the process are, firstly, the variable amount of principal that can be repaid each month, secondly, the

---

[130] In 2005, monthly payments on structured securities, occurring on the 25th of each month, surpassed the $50 billion mark. ('Structured Securities Processing Challenges', DTCC, June 2006).

high proportion of structured securities for which the monthly payment amount is not known until the day payment is due and, thirdly, the relatively large number of payments to holders that have to be adjusted retrospectively. Recently, DTC has been able to push forward the deadline for payment information from paying agents to 11.30pm on the day before payment. DTC has also proposed an "exception processing fee" for structured securities that have been created in such a complex manner that the paying agents cannot make the new deadline.[131]

There is one further category of corporate action for holders of CDOs. Known as **events of default** (EODs) these include failure to pay interest, or repay principal, or the bankruptcy of the SPV. The structure that gives structured securities their name is a division of the risk involved into different 'tranches'. In the event of the bankruptcy of the SPV each tranche receives different treatment. The most senior tranche would have the first claim on the liquidated assets of the CDO and the claim of the next most senior tranche can only be met out of what remains. At the bottom of the pile is what is known as the "first loss piece" tranche, sometimes known as the "equity piece" whose holders will be expecting very high rates of interest for the risks they are exposed to.[132]

Since summer 2007 the higher rates of default on subprime mortgages have added a further strain to the processing of payments on structured securities. These processing problems may have contributed to the problems that some major banks have had in placing an accurate valuation on the asset backed securities that they hold and the consequent delays in subprime losses coming to light.

---

[131] DTCC press releases 2007. Also 'Transforming Structured Securities Processing', DTCC, September 2007. The exception processing fee, due to be introduced in 2008, was expected to be in the region of $4,200. DTCC reckoned that this "non-conforming" status would apply to some 3,600 instruments, about 7.5% of the total number of issues, which account for about 50% of the total number of late payment rate submissions. The exception processing fee received authorisation from the SEC in late March 2008.

[132] This process is euphemistically termed a "waterfall structure".

Securities lending and corporate actions

The practice of (equity) securities lending by investment funds is another area on which corporate actions impinge.[133] Some funds manage their own securities lending programme while others out-source the task to custodian banks. The task of liaison with stock borrowers over corporate actions is the most demanding element in administering a lending programme. The key principle in regard to corporate actions is that the entitlement passes to the borrower at the time, but it is normal for the lender to expect to have the benefit of corporate actions once they receive them back.[134] Securities lending contracts will make detailed provision for corporate event situations. For example, the contract may stipulate whether, in a takeover for the stock in question, the borrower has to follow the instructions of the lender or, alternatively, return the stock to the lender.

Some companies' stock is more in demand by borrowers than others'. This is as a consequence of specific corporate actions being anticipated, such as dividend payments or takeover bids. In the securities lending market these are known as "specials".

Shareholder votes pose a particular problem to funds involved in securities lending as the lender will have recall the stock if they wish to vote at a shareholder meeting.[135] Lenders who recall securities in order

---

[133] Much of the demand for stock lending comes from hedge funds, but these often use their prime broker to act as the counterparty in the contract. Broker dealers may use borrowed securities for their market making role. Securities lending may also be used to work around withholding taxes for offshore investors so that, for example, an offshore holder of a German security might engage in lending to avoid the 25% German withholding tax.

[134] The entitlement to corporate actions in the context of lent securities derives from the legal basis of the transaction; strictly speaking, this is a transfer of the security with an undertaking that the borrower will return the exact equivalent securities.

[135] See 'Review of the impediments to voting UK shares', report by Paul Myners to the Shareholder Voting Working Group (SVWG) and 'Review of Securities Lending and Corporate Governance', Mark Faulkner, Spitalfields Advisors.

to vote very frequently may deter borrowers. As a result lenders tend either not to recall at all or to do so in the event of highly important EGMs. EGMs, for example, where the outcome desired by the securities lender is not a foregone conclusion.

Corporate actions and investment strategies

Hedge funds' appetite for borrowing "specials" is an example of an investment strategy based on the potential for gains arising from corporate actions. Such funds may be on the look out for corporate event situations in general, or in some cases develop specialist expertise in spotting arbitrage opportunities arising from just one type of corporate action (for example, takeovers).

At the level of the individual investor, intelligent interpretation of event situations can be used in conjunction with investment theories. For instance, investors using technical analysis of share prices may also keep a watch for corporate actions that are likely to trigger re-ratings in the stocks they are focusing on. In watching for these actions they equip the "invisible hand" of the market with squeaky shoes or a tapping cane to alert investors to opportunities.

Investors on any scale who are taking advantage of stockbroker's stop loss facilities (or similar) should check if and how the provider of this service will make adjustments for corporate actions happening while the stop loss is in place.[136] For example, without an adjustment being made to the stop loss, a return of capital by the issuer might trigger the stop loss into the sale of the investor's holding.

---

[136] These include facilities for limit orders, range trading and price locking.

And other stakeholders

Occasions when other corporate stakeholders have an observable or quantifiable effect on corporate actions are infrequent. After all, it is the job of the company's board of directors to reconcile the competing interests of different stakeholders in preparation for submitting proposals to shareholders. Pressure to amend or reverse directors' recommendations or decisions on corporate actions undermines confidence in the board.

The most serious recent instance of a derailed corporate action was the abandonment of plans for a dividend payment by Northern Rock shortly after the run on the bank in September 2007. The generous 14.2p a share interim dividend (an increase of 30% on the previous year's) had been announced in July, following the publication of the interim results. Pressure to cancel the dividend came from the government since taxpayers were clearly major stakeholders in the business following the bail out. The move was a clear signal that the board's powers were held on sufferance.

The cancellation of the Northern Rock dividend is unlikely to be the start of a trend in overturning corporate actions, but there is a long-term growth of concern on their effect on the best interests of one stakeholder group; pension fund members. Trustees of pension funds have already begun to see their role as one of protecting the interests of what is often, in effect, a company's largest unsecured creditor. In the UK the Pensions Act 2004 introduced higher standards of scheme funding and increased employer liabilities for funding.

In relation to equity corporate actions, a pension scheme's ability to meet its liabilities may be adversely affected by any event that reduces shareholders' funds, that changes corporate control, that affects the ratio of company assets to pension liabilities, or earnings to employer's pension contributions. The following corporate actions could trigger such circumstances:

- Re-organisations
- Divestments
- Takeovers
- Reductions in capital
- Share buybacks
- Dividends

Although it would not impinge directly on shareholders' entitlements, an increase in the level of security offered to creditors would also be of concern to a fund's trustees.

In recent years the issue of pension scheme finance has been a significant factor in the success or failure of a number of high profile takeover bids such as those for Boots, Corus, Marks & Spencer, J Sainsbury and WHSmith.

All above board

By their nature corporate actions are not deeds done in the dark but are open to scrutiny, by shareholders, first and foremost, but also by the investment industry as a whole and financial commentators. Nor should the role of tax inspectors in keeping everything above board be forgotten. This does not mean that participants in the corporate actions process are completely invulnerable to abuse. For example, there have been allegations of custodian nominee accounts being used for secret transfers of securities, and that ICSDs have given unpublished accounts to some clients that were then used for movements of cash rather than the settling of securities transactions.

Generally speaking, while securities can be used for money laundering or bribery, no one has yet seemed able to devise a way to do so and to benefit from the corporate action entitlements of ownership.

13.

Conclusion

After the dotcom bubble there was a retreat in investment and development in equity settlement. The Global Straight Through Processing Association (disolved towards the end of 2002) was the most high-profile casualty. In the corporate actions processing industry there were cutbacks in investment, too. DTCC's plans for a Global Corporate Actions Hub (the GCAH) were laid aside in the second half of 2003.[137] Now, in the wake of the huge debt security write-downs since summer 2007, the likelihood is that the processing of debt securities corporate actions will experience at least an equal measure of retrenchment in the next year or two.

How corporate actions will develop in the next few years depends upon what kinds of investment products are likely to be most attractive. At the time of writing the front running candidate seems to be commodities. A continuing boom in just commodities (which have no corporate actions) implies a quieter time for the corporate actions processing industry. Short-term economies will probably be the order of the day and this may mean increasing numbers of financial institutions outsourcing their corporate actions work.

For equity corporate actions change and growth looks most likely to arise in countries like China and India. However, corporate actions are unlikely to simply track the growth of those economies or their stock markets. In China in particular, speculation seems to be the prime motivator for investment with private investors preferring scrip dividends to cash ones. A longer-term perspective on the state share reform process is needed in order to know whether or not Chinese issuers will consistently handle corporate actions in the same way as companies based in Europe or

---

[137] The GCAH was intended to be a standardised messaging system for the industry. The scheme died a quiet death and no detailed explanation was ever given. The most likely causes were the hostility of vendors of corporate actions information and the unwillingness of investment funds, stockbrokers and custodians to subscribe to an extra service.

North America. This will be one of the most significant developments to watch out for, for both Chinese and foreign investors.

Whatever progress globalisation makes in financial markets, as far as corporate actions are concerned, it looks as if local practices will be continuing for a long time to come.

So far no adverse judgments have been made on the role of corporate actions processing while the structured securities market plunged off the rails. Most institutions seem to have paid little heed to events of default even on the lower tranches of structured securities, let alone on the senior debt that constituted the bulk of these investments. Looking back, these non-payment events should have been spotted as early warning signs of problems ahead for the senior debt of the securities in question. Corporate actions processing systems were working harder and faster to cope with structured securities payment events and resources do not seem to have allowed for full analysis of events of default data. In the future, the payment events of securities that are supposed to spread risk probably deserve to receive closer attention.

Generally, corporate actions deserve more attention from the financial press. As mentioned in Chapter 4, there is very little comment about the approach of different investment banks in the advice they give to issuers about almost any corporate action except mergers and acquisitions. There is also a noticeable absence of discussion of corporate actions in the context of the debate about corporate governance. This tends to focus on subjects such as directors remuneration and conflicts of interest within accountancy firms, but corporate actions can be a good indicator. More publicity about the record of corporate action entitlements accruing from the investments that listed companies make would be particularly welcome.[138]

---

[138] The absence of this kind of information was, after all, one of the reasons for the downfall of Enron.

Glossary

acceleration covenant

Allows for the early redemption of a bond in the event of certain specified circumstances such as a downgrade by the rating agencies.

accrued interest

With debt securities the element of the dirty price that is interest; the accrued interest matches the proportion of the time between coupon dates that has been reached at the time of purchase.

advance warning plan

(In Japan) A standing takeover defence plan that allows a company to demand information from a predator about its intentions. If the target company is not satisfied with the response it may issue warrants to all its other shareholders.

agent bank

Another name for a bank providing securities custody services.

alarm bell report

Notice by a Central Securities Depository that a deadline for a corporate action is approaching. Euroclear will normally send a member an alarm bell report two working days before the deadline and one working day beforehand.

asset backed securities

Debt securities with a pool of assets earmarked to provide income to meet the coupon.

beneficial owner

The individual or corporation that enjoys the entitlements of owning a security as opposed to the registered holder.

bond indenture

The contract between an issuer and purchasers stipulating the terms of a corporate bond. Also known as a bond agreement.

bonus issue

An issue of extra shares in proportion to shareholders' existing holdings at no extra charge. The effect is to reduce retained earnings in proportion to the share capital of the company in question. Also known as a capitalisation issue.

bonus share plan

Shares issued from the issuer's share premium reserve and qualifying as a capital distribution rather than income under Australian tax legislation.

broker votes

(Chiefly in the US) Voting by brokers when instructions from beneficial owners have not been received by the deadline. Exchange rules prevent brokers voting in some contentious areas.

bullet

Repayment of debt in a single sum.

busted convertible

A convertible security for which the share price of the underlying share is so low that conversion is never likely to take place. Busted status is normally deemed to have been achieved when the share price sinks below 50% of the share price signified by the security's conversion rate.

callable bonds

Bonds that allow for optional early redemption at the behest of the issuer.

call (or pre-payment) provisions

The terms that a bond indenture sets for the "in whole" or partial redemption of the bond.

call protection

A period at the beginning of the life of a bond when the investor is protected from the issuer exercising the option of early redemption.

capital gains distribution

(In the US) A payment to investment fund investors of profits realised on the sale of securities.

capitalisation issue

This can be just an alternative name for a bonus issue. However "capitalisation issue" is a term that is sometimes used to describe a one-off wholesale replacement of a dividend with an issue of shares.

capped FRN

A floating rate note with a ceiling on the maximum interest payable.

class test provisions

The four categories of corporate transaction under the UK Listing Rule 10; Class 1 (the biggest) transactions require shareholder approval before going ahead.

clearing

The establishment of a contractual obligation between the buyer and seller of a security.

collateral trust certificate

A kind of covered bond where the assets backing the issue are normally the securities of the issuer's subsidiaries.

common stock

Ordinary shares of a company entitling the investor to vote at shareholder meetings, receive a (variable) dividend and share in the capital appreciation of the company.

(share) consolidation

The replacement of a company's existing stock by a smaller number of shares with a higher value, but with no change to the total value of the shares in issue.

conversion

A (convertible) bond becoming another kind of debt security or an ordinary share (or shares). The conversion rate is normally stipulated at the time of issue.

convertible loan stock

Debt security that is convertible into the ordinary shares of the issuer; convertible loan stock is tradable and the price reflects fluctuations in the share price. Convertible unsecured loan stock (CULS) is a variation of this.

corporate actions liability notices

These notify the previous owner of a share that the current owner has not yet received the shares in settlement. Typically the notices are sent out when a voluntary corporate action is about to take place and the current owner is unable to make their election because the settlement is not yet complete.

corporate bond

Bonds issued by companies and normally carrying a higher coupon than government bonds.

corporate nominee

The (unusual) practice of an issuer providing a custody service for holders of its shares, normally used to smooth the way for new shareholders in a demutualisation.

cost base / cost basis

The "floor" above which a taxable capital gain from a sale of shares is calculated.

coupon

The interest payable on a bond, derived from the coupon that had to be presented to the issuer for payment to be made. The coupon date is the payment date.

covered bond

A bond or loan note that is backed by other assets so that, in the event of the issuer going into liquidation, the purchasers have a claim on the underlying assets.

covered warrant

Warrants for which the issuer holds the underlying shares to match the purchaser's entitlement if they opt to exercise their right to shares.

CREST

The UK share settlement system inaugurated in July 1996. Originally owned by CRESTCo, now Euroclear UK & Ireland. CREST is not an acronym. The CREST Blue Book sets out corporate actions standards and norms for payment of dividends and interest.

cumulative voting

A voting regime that allows minority shareholders to concentrate their votes in elections of directors on one candidate. For example, if four directorships were up for election they could use four votes in favour of a candidate for just one directorship. (see also "short slate").

custodian nominee

A company through which a custodian bank holds shares in custody (to keep shareholdings held in trust separate from its own assets).

data scrubbing

The work of verifying corporate actions notices to ensure smooth and accurate processing.

de-materialised

Shares existing only in electronic as opposed to certificated form (when a physical share certificate exists).

Depository Trust Company

The depository component of DTCC.

dilution

Reduction in existing shareholders shareholdings as a proportion of the total shares in issue.

dilution protection

A benefit to holders of convertible bonds whereby bonus issues or scrip dividends above a certain proportion (5% is common) trigger an increase of the conversion ratio of the bond.

dirty price

The actual price paid for bonds, which includes the interest accrued since the previous coupon date.

discretionary portfolio

Service offered by stockbrokers and financial advisers where all the share dealing decisions are put into effect without referring back to the owner of the portfolio.

divisor

The number used in the calculation of stock exchange indices that ensures comparability over time. The divisor is re-calculated for all changes in the shares in issue for constituents of the index. Every share split or share consolidation will necessitate a recalculation of the divisor.

drawing

As an alternative to partial redemption according to a preordained schedule, the practice of selecting bonds to be redeemed by lot.

DRIPs

Dividend Reinvestment Plan, a purchase of shares funded by some or all of the dividend payable to the investor.

drop-lock FRN

A floating rate note that converts to a fixed rate security if interest rates drop to a specified level.

entitlement offer

More commonly referred to as an "open offer".

event interpretation grid

The 'grid' is a reference tool (in spreadsheet format) for applying ISO 15022 standardised messages in a uniform manner across different jurisdictions.

events of default

EODs are a failure of the issuer of a debt security (especially structured securities) to meet the purchasers' entitlements such as an interest payment or repayment of principal.

excess application

In open offers, a device for enabling shareholders to apply for a higher proportion of an issue than their existing shareholding entitles them to. The issuer counts all the applications it receives before deciding whether to meet all the applications in full or to scale them back.

excessive dividend

A dividend that is excessive in relation to the company's capitalisation, cash flow or general financial position, and/or is being used as a means of dissolving the company. Depending on the company law of the country of domicile of the company, excessive dividends can be reclaimed.

exchange offer

An offer of one security in exchange for another, typically as part of a takeover. A securities exchange offer is one where the predator/acquirer offers any security of its own except its loan stock or loan notes.

exempt distribution

Treating a distribution of shares in a de-merger as if the (now) two companies were still one company reorganising its share capital. In the UK section 213 of the Income and Corporation Taxes Act 1988 sets out the requirements that must be met to gain exemption.

extendable bond

Allow the issuer to postpone the redemption date (nb, some definitions of "extendable bond" place the initiative with the holder rather than the issuer).

fixed interest securities

This term looks self-explanatory but can be ambivalent. In this guide it is taken to mean securities with an unvarying coupon rate but, sometimes it is used merely to signify securities with predetermined rates of interest or as a synonym for bonds in general.

floating rate note

Securities for which the rate of interest payable fluctuates at a determined level relative to a reference interest rate.

fully-paid rights

A rights issue share for which payment in full has been made to the issuer. Trading in the fully paid shares normally commences a few days after the deadline for full payment.

gearing ratio covenant

In the terms of a bond indenture, the level of other borrowings permitted to an issuer in the lifetime of the bond before an early redemption is triggered.

global custodian

A bank providing securities custody services for all markets, either directly or through arrangements with "sub-custodians".

golden record

In corporate actions processing, an announcement that is completely reliable, the information having been checked against more than one source.

guaranteed bond

Where the principal and/or the interest payments are guaranteed by a corporation that is not the issuer.

hybrid securities

Unsecured subordinated debt securities that regulators and credit rating agencies may treat a part of the issuers capital (although it is debt rather than equity and has corporate actions to match).

immobilised

Shares held by a Central Securities Depository are said to be immobilised as there is no need for them to be moved when they change hands; the transfer is recorded by book entry at the CSD.

impairment charge

A balance sheet reduction to reflect a downward adjustment in goodwill. Such a charge could cause a company to breach covenants on debt.

institutional loan stock

Venture capital loan, which may or may not be secured.

ISO 15022

The International standard for electronic messaging in the securities industry. The Society for Worldwide Interbank Financial Telecommunications (SWIFT) was the standard's sponsor and continues to be the Registration Authority. ISO 20022 is the latest standard for the industry with more areas covered and mandating use of XML.

issuer

The organisation that places a security in the market.

LDR

Last Date of Registration (for elections in corporate actions).

lead manager

An investment bank that takes the primary responsibility in an issue of securities and, in particular, takes the lead role if the issue is underwritten by a syndicate of banks.

letter of transmittal

A form used in the United States as a requirement of the IRS where shares being held in material form are being sold or exchanged.

loan note

A method of paying for acquisitions through borrowing. The use of loan notes may be attractive to shareholders in a target company if they wish to postpone realising a capital gain. Loan notes are transferable.

margin ratchet

A reduction in the margin on a loan facility triggered by certain targets being met. Margin ratchets feature in management buyouts.

master servicer

For structured securities the master servicer is responsible for supervising the collection of mortgage payments by primary servicers and passing funds to the trustee, for reporting to holders of the security on the performance of the assets and appointing a special servicer when assets become non-performing.

mezzanine finance

Debt that would be paid off after senior debt, but before instituted loan stock, in the event of a liquidation. It is likely to have warrants or be convertible.

mini-max FRN

A floating rate note with lower and upper limits on the range in which the rate of interest payable can fluctuate.

mix and match election

A company making a takeover bid may offer shareholders the option to take the consideration for their shares in a mixture of cash and the offerer's shares. The offer has no effect on the total amounts of cash and shares used in the takeover; the acquirer is only obliging to the extent that shareholders with a preference for cash can be matched with those with a preference for the stock.

mortgage backed securities (MBS)

Asset backed securities where the assets are all comprised of (residential) mortgages. Where the mortgages are on commercial property, they would be known as commercial MBS.

municipal bond

In the US a bond issued by a city, county, state or other government body for public works projects. The interest payable is often free of tax

naked warrant

Warrants for which the issuer does not hold the underlying shares to match the purchasers entitlement if they opt to exercise their right to shares.

near miss

A phrase borrowed from air traffic control by practitioners in corporate actions attempting to gauge the scale of risks and impact of (potential) mistakes.

negative pledge

In the terms of a bond indenture, a negative pledge prevents the issuer from pledging greater collateral or security to another lender.

nil-paid rights

A short-lived tradable security consisting of the rights to buy a (rights issue) share at its fully-paid price.

omnibus nominee

A custodian's nominee that holds the accounts of more than one client. This practice is common. The opposite would be a nominee account with a "specific designation".

open offer

An issue of new shares without tradable nil-paid rights. *See*, also, "excess application".

pari passu

Securities that are identical in all respects (see also, - fungible). The expression is normally used when shares with different dividend entitlements or voting rights become identical.

partial redemption

Under the terms of a bond indenture, a bond may have provisions for staged repayment of the principal and reductions in the interest payable.

partly paid

Shares that are only partly paid for with the issuer choosing the times for balance to be paid in what are known as "instalment calls".

pay if you can (PIYC)

Interest payments that accumulate until a certain cash flow level triggers a payment.

paying agent

Plays a custody role in structured securities, issuing certificates and acting as a channel for the payments due to investors.

payment in kind (PIK)

A somewhat misleading term for interest that accumulates on debt securities and is repaid at a specified date or when a company is sold.

performance ratchet

Also known as an equity ratchet. Terms in the buyout of a company to increase the owner managers' stake if certain targets are met. Normally, the terms of the ratchet will be added to the articles of association.

pre-emption right

The right to participate in an issue of new shares in proportion to the investor's existing shareholding.

preference shares

Shares that are treated preferentially in two ways: their dividend (which is normally fixed) is paid ahead of any dividend on common stock and they take precedence over common stock in the event of the issuer going into liquidation. Preference shares normally do not carry voting rights.

proportional takeover bid

A proportional takeover bid is a takeover bid where the offer made to each shareholder is only for a proportion of that shareholder's shares (ie, less than 100%).

provisional allotment letters

These show a shareholder's entitlement to shares in a rights issue. A shareholder who wished to take up some of their rights but not all would "split" the allotment letter, an effect normally achieved using a covering letter.

puttable bonds

Bonds with optional early redemption at the instigation of the investor.

re-chaining

The process of making adjustments to stock charts to ensure that they allow for changes in share price that have arisen through corporate actions such as bonus issues or consolidations. This means projecting backwards what the share price would have been if the number of shares in issue had been at the current level since the chart began.

redemption

The repayment of the principal by the issuer of a debt security.

Regulatory News Service (RNS)

The announcements service of the London Stock Exchange.

relative dividend yield

A comparison of a single company's dividend yield with the dividend of the market (or index) as a whole. Some investors favour this ratio as a criterion for stock selection. Relative dividend yields are available on sites such as **www.Bloomberg.com.**

reset date

The date when the interest on a floating rate note is changed.

residual assets

Assets remaining after the claims of all holders of senior debt have been met.

retail investor

A private individual investing through a stockbroker, not an investor in a retail investment fund.

return of capital

A reduction of the number of shares in issue with a return of cash to shareholders. Returns of capital are often achieved by an exchange of shares with the shareholder receiving back fewer ordinary shares but also some 'B' shares that the issuer promises to redeem for cash at a future date.

reverse takeover

The acquisition of a larger company by a smaller one or the acquisition of a listed company by an unlisted one (in order to obtain a stock market listing).

scheme of arrangement

A court sanctioned agreement between a company and its shareholders and/or its creditors for changes to its securities. Schemes of arrangement can be made for rescheduling debt, takeovers or returns of capital.

scrip dividend reference price

(When calculating scrip dividend entitlements) A divisor applied to the cash dividend entitlement to work out how many shares the cash dividend equates to. The scrip dividend reference price will always be a reading of the issuer's share price according to a formula announced well beforehand.

secondary market

The ordinary market in which investors purchase shares from one another, as opposed to the primary market, where the shares are purchased from the issuer at the time of issue. The usefulness of the distinction as far as private investors are concerned is questionable.

securities exchange offer

(*see* exchange offer)

sell out (rights)

The right of a shareholder in a company that has been taken over to have their stake bought out by the acquiring company at a fair price.

senior debt

Borrowing from a bank that is normally secured and that takes preference over other borrowings in the event of liquidation.

separate register

Separate registers of shares are maintained as legal requirements. For example, the shareholdings of directors and close family members will be maintained in one. Some countries or jurisdictions require separate registers of foreigners' shareholdings if the company is considered strategically important for the security or economy of the country or region in question.

servicer

Also known as primary servicers or sub-servicers; responsible for ensuring that the payments due on the assets of a structured security are collected.

settlement

The transfer of securities from the seller to the buyer and the transfer of funds from the buyer to the seller.

share blocking

The requirement that exists in some countries for shares not to be traded around the time of a shareholder vote. Share blocking may be mandated in a country's company law, but could equally be permitted by law but mandated in an individual company's articles.

share buyback

An exercise in which a company buys its own shares on the open market.

share placing

Best defined by saying what it is not: viz. an offering of shares to the public in a company flotation or an offer of new shares to existing shareholders in a rights issue or open offer. A share placing would normally be with a private equity house or investment bank. A "private placing" is one where the company in question does not have a stock market listing.

share register

Maintaining a register of shares is a legal requirement of all companies that issue shares traded on public exchanges. The share registrar role is normally outsourced.

share split

See "bonus issue".

short slate

In the US SEC rules have allowed dissident shareholders to nominate a director or directors by indicating which management nominees they are withholding their votes from.

SMPG

Securities Market Practice Group – there are around 30 of these groups around the world, to which the implementation of messaging standards (see ISO 15022) in corporate actions have been devolved.

solicitation of shareholders' consent

A procedure that aims to obtain shareholders' consent to proposals (by the issuer or a third party) that would otherwise require a formal general meeting.

special dividend

Any dividend that is outside an issuer's normal pattern of dividends (and interim dividends).

special purpose vehicle (SPV)

May be a subsidiary company established in a different country to take advantage of a more benign tax regime.

In relation to debt securities an SPV is an organisation with the specific purpose of holding legal rights over assets for an issuer.

specials

In the context of stock lending "specials" are stocks that are particularly attractive because of upcoming corporate actions (such as a good dividend payment or a takeover).

specific designation

A custodian's nominee with the holdings of a single client is known as a 'nominee with a specific designation'. This makes contacting beneficial owners easier and helps to improve levels of proxy voting.

squeeze out

The right for an acquiring company to buy out minority shareholders. Under EU law squeeze out rights come into effect when the acquirer has 90-95% of the target company's shares (the precise threshold is set at the discretion of individual member states).

statutory consolidation

A corporate merger where the merging companies lose all of their separate identities.

step-up bonds

Bonds paying one rate of interest for an initial period and a specified higher rate from a certain date.

stock dividend

(In the US) Another name for a "scrip dividend".

stock situation notice

A notice of a corporate action affecting a quoted company; specifically, such an announcement in the Corporate Events Diary of the London Stock Exchange.

STP

Straight Through Processing; the watchword for advocates of standardisation in corporate actions.

structured securities

Debt securities, such as collateralised debt obligations, that are structured into separate tranches with differing degrees of risk exposure for the holders of each tranche.

sub-custodian

A bank that participates in a Central Securities Depository and is therefore able to provide a custody service to global custodians in that particular market.

subscription rights

See "pre-emption right".

succession event

Buyouts, de-mergers or spin-offs may leave holders of some kinds of debt securities exposed to greater risk, or less clear about the degree of risk they are exposed to. A corporate action that brings about this kind of change of regime is known as a succession event.

SWIFT

Society for Worldwide Interbank Financial Telecommunication – in the context of corporate actions, SWIFT is the chief promoter of standardised (ISO) messaging standards.

total return

The combination of the returns from a share (such as the dividend, return of capital, profit from trading nil-paid rights) and the share's appreciation in price on the stock market.

transter agent

Share registrar in North America.

transfer secretary

Share registrar in southern African countries.

treasury shares

The issuer's own shares paid for out of profits and held by the treasury department rather than being cancelled.

TTE

This stands for "transfer to escrow". The term frequently appears in documentation sent to shareholders by issuers as in "TTE instructions", which refers to elections shareholders choose to make about an entitlement that is not yet their's (and is therefore in escrow).

uncertificated shares

Shares whose existence is only recorded on computer (dematerialised).

unconditional offer

The stage when a takeover offer ceases to be contingent upon more shareholders accepting the offer (ie, when the acquirer has achieved the target for acceptances set out in the offer document).

warrant

A tradable instrument that gives the holder the optional right to shares in the issuing company at a specified date. Corporate bonds are sometimes issued with warrants attached.

Appendices

List of Central Securities Depositories

Some countries have more than one CSD listed; central/national banks or other agencies often act as the CSD for government bonds and some countries (eg, Russia and the UK) have separate arrangements for short-term money market instruments. In the table below the body acting as a central depository for equities is in bold type; these organizations may also be depositories for some or all other kinds of security.

Country	Name of Depository
Argentina	**Caja de Valores S.A.**
Australia	Austraclear Ltd
	Clearing House Electronic Subregister System
	Reserve Bank Information and Transfer System
Austria	**Oesterreichische Kontrollbank AG**
Belgium	**Euroclear Belgium**
	Banque Nationale de Belgique
Brazil	Camara de Liquidacao e Custodia S.A. (CLC)
	Companhia Brasileira de Liquidaco e Custodia (CBLC)
Bulgaria	**The Central Depository AD (CDAD)**
Canada	**Canadian Depository for Securities Ltd**
Chile	**Deposito Central de Valores S.A.**
China	**Shanghai Securities Central Clearing and Registration Corp.**
	Shenzhen Securities Central Clearing Company Ltd
Costa Rica	**Central de Valores de la Bolsa Nacional de Valores S.A. (CEVAL)**
Czech Republic	**UNIVYC**
	St edisko Cenných Papír
	Czech National Bank

Denmark	**Vaerdipapircentralen (VP) (The Danish Securities Centre)**
Egypt	**Misr. Central Securities Depository (MCSD)**
Estonia	**Estonia Central Securities Depository (ECSDL)**
Finland	**The Finnish Central Securities Depository Ltd** (Arvopaperikeskus – APK, part of the Nordic Central Securities Depository)
France	**Euroclear France**
Germany	**Clearstream, part of Deutsche Börse**
Greece	**Apothetirion Titlon AE (The Central Securities Depository)**
	Bank of Greece
Hong Kong	Central Moneymarkets Unit (CMU), Hong Kong Monetary Authority
	The Central Clearing and Settlement System, Hong Kong Securities Clearing Company
Hungary	**Kozponti Elszamolohaz es Ertektar Rt. (KELER – Central Clearing House and Depository)**
India	**National Securities Depository Ltd (NSDL)**
	The Reserve Bank of India
	Central Depository Services Ltd
Indonesia	**PT Kustodian Sentral Efek Indonesia**
	Bank of Indonesia
Ireland	CRESTCo. Ltd
Israel	**The Tel Aviv Stock Exchange Clearing House**
	The Bank of Israel
Italy	**Monte Titoli, part of Borsa Italiana**
Ivory Coast	**Ivory Coast Central Depository**
Japan	Bank of Japan
	Japan Securities Depository Center
Kazakhstan	**Central Depository of Securities (CJSC)**
Korea	**Korean Securities Depository Corp.**
Latvia	**The Latvian Central Depository (LCD)**
	Bank of Latvia

Lebanon	**Midclear**
	Banque du Liban
Lithuania	**Lietuvus Centrinis Vertybiniv Popieriv Depozitoriumas (Central Securities Depository of Lithuania)**
Luxembourg	**Clearstream, formerly Cedel Bank, S.A.**
Malaysia	**The Malaysian Central Depository Sdn. Bhd.**
	Scripless Securities Trading and Safekeeping System
	Bank Negara
Malta	**Central Securities Depository**
Mauritius	**The Central Depository & Settlement Company Ltd**
Mexico	**Instituto para el Depósito de Valores (INDEVAL)**
	Banco de Mexico
Morocco	**Maroclear**
	Centrale des Titres Scripturaux
Netherlands	**Euroclear Nederland (formerly Nederlands Centraal Instituut voor Giraal Effectenverkeer BV)**
New Zealand	**Central Securities Depository Ltd (NZCSD)**
Norway	**Verdipapirsentralen (Norwegian Registry of Securities - VPS)**
Oman	**Muscat Depository and Transfer Co. (MDTC)**
Pakistan	**Central Depository Company of Pakistan, Ltd**
Peru	**Caja de Valores y Liquidaciones (CAVALI)**
Philippines	Bangko Sentral ng Philipinas
	Philippines Central Depository
Poland	**Krajowy Depozyt Papierow Wartosciowych (National Depository for Securities)**
	Centralny Rejestr Bonow Skarbowych, Central Treasury Bills Registrar (CTBR)
Portugal	**Interbolsa**
Romania	**Depozitarul Centra**
Russia	**Depositary Clearing Company**
	National Depository Center
	Bank of Foreign trade

Singapore	**The Central Depository Pte. Ltd**
	Monetary Authority of Singapore (MAS)
Slovakia	**Centrálny depozitár cenných papierov**
	National Bank of Slovakia
Slovenia	**Centralna Klirinsko Depotna Druzba (Central Securities Clearing Corporation – KDD)**
South Africa	**Strate**
Spain	**Iberclear**
Sri Lanka	**The Central Depository Systems (Pvt.) Ltd**
Sweden	**Vardepapperscentralen (VPC), part of the Nordic Central Securities Depository**
Switzerland	SIS SegaInterSettle
Taiwan	**Taiwan Securities Central Depository Co. Ltd**
	Central Bank of China
Thailand	**Thailand Securities Depository Co. Ltd**
Turkey	**Takasbank**
	Central Bank of Turkey
UK	United Kingdom Central Gilts Office - Bank of England
	Central Moneymarkets Office - Bank of England (for short-dated instruments)
	CRESTCo. Ltd
USA	**Depository Trust Company**
	Participant Trust Company
	Federal Reserve Bank
Venezuela	Caja de Valores (CVV Venezolana)

Capital Gains Tax Example – Biffa/Severn Trent

This example uses the figures given for the spin-off of Biffa from Severn Trent PLC in Chapter 2. It is assumed that the investor has realised the capital gain through selling both the Biffa shares and the Severn Trent shares on 30th November 2007 (and therefore will be taxed according to the CGT rates applying in the tax year 2007/8).

The shareholder in the example has acquired 375 shares in Biffa as a result of the spin-off and 250 Severn Trent shares in the two-for-three share consolidation. To work out the cost base for these shares requires a record of the date on which the shares were originally acquired (say, for the purposes of this illustration, 30th September 2005) and the proportion of the original share stake that was transformed into Biffa shares one year later.

The purchase cost of the Severn Trent shares in 2005 was 1043.8p a share, giving the share stake a value of £3,914.25. This is the previous base cost.

The next stage in the calculation is to find out what proportion of your holding was transformed into Biffa shares:

Biffa shares (375 x 260p) = £975

and what proportion remained as Severn Trent shares (albeit consolidated).[139] The market value of the consolidated shares on 9th October 2006 was 1,440p a share:

Severn Trent shares (250 x 1,440p) = £3,600

---

[139] Share consolidation calculations are likely to produce a left over fraction of a share. In this case any shareholding of Severn Trent shares that was not exactly divisible by three would have left the shareholder with a fraction of a share that was dealt with by paying cash.

The Biffa shares had a value equal to 21.3% of the combined Biffa and Severn Trent shareholdings on 9th October 2006:[140]

The cost base of the 250 new shares received in Severn Trent PLC is £3,080:

£3,914.25 x 78.7% =   **£3,080**

The cost base date for the Biffa shares is £834:

£3,914.25 x 21.3% =   **£834**[141]

The price the Biffa shares were sold for on 30th November 2007 was 333p a share, grossing £1,249.[142] The total taxable gain is £415 (for the sake of simplicity assume that the investor has already used up their capital gains tax allowance).

The Severn Trent shares were worth 1,567p a share on the same day, grossing £3,918. This would have produced a taxable gain of £838.

Help from HM Revenue & Customs

HM Revenue and Customs publish helpsheets to assist with CGT calculations on shares which can be accessed online at **www.hmrc.gov.uk/helpsheets**. These are particularly useful for the "bed & breakfast", pooling and matching rules. Issuers will normally provide notes on the tax positions arising from corporate actions such as returns of capital or de-mergers, to help maintain good investor relations.

---

[140] The special dividend that was also paid as part of the consolidation/de-merger exercise appears to have been treated entirely as an income distribution subject to income tax. Consequently, it plays no part in the cost base calculations.

[141] Note that online dealing services' portfolio valuation screens should show the cost base of the shares in the spun off company, not their share price on the first day of trading.

[142] Biffa shares had been down on price on the first day of trading for most of 2007 but Montagu Private Equity and HGCapital made a second (higher) bid approach for the company at the end of November 2007.

Non-rights Issues of Shares

In the UK companies wishing to issue equity other than by means of a rights issue have the following methods to choose from:

1. Cash Placing

Under the pre-emption rules these are limited to 5% of issued share capital in any year, or 7.5% in a rolling three-year period. The rules only allow a discount to the price of existing shares of 5%.[143]

2. Vendor Placing

These occur in acquisitions such as the purchase of another company's subsidiary. In the event that the vendor wishes to receive cash for their divestment, the acquiring company has the option, under the pre-emption rules, of selling shares to third parties up to the level of 10% of issued share capital.

3. Cashbox Placing

Another placing method that is normally only used in the context of acquisitions. The cashbox (B) is a subsidiary of the listed company (A) seeking to issue more shares. B's shares will be subscribed to or underwritten by A's investment bank. Company A will then issue shares to B with B's cash as the consideration. This cash can then be used to finance A's takeover activities.

---

[143] The pre-emption rules are the guidelines of the Pre-emption Group and derive their force from the willingness of the Association of British Insurers and the National Association of Pension Funds to uphold them. Shareholders' legally enforceable pre-emption rights are set out in the Companies Act 2006 and provide a lower barrier to non-rights share issues than the pre-emption rules.

4. Open Offers

Open offers do come with subscription rights for shareholders. The difference from a true rights issue is that open offers do not include a tradable entitlement to buy the rights.

5. Directors' Authority to Allot Shares

Many companies, especially large ones, may propose resolutions at annual general meetings that renew the directors' authority to allot securities for cash to the shareholders and to sell Treasury shares. This enables them to move quickly to acquire new backing and fresh capital (as has been necessary for a number of banks that have turned to private equity and sovereign wealth funds in recent months). This could be seen as pre-empting pre-emption.[144]

Pre-emption rights do not exist for shareholders in US corporations. They are present in the corporate law of all the larger European Union economies though, and are enshrined in the European Union's Second Company Law Directive (77/91/EEC).[145] However, current opinion seems to be in favour of loosening EU legislation in this area.[146]

Australia and Canada have pre-emption rights but allow larger non pre-emptive share issues than European countries permit (up to 25% of issued shares in a six month period in the case of Canada). Japan has no pre-emption rights but issues of discounted shares require the approval of 66% of shareholders represented at a general meeting.

---

[144] In the UK the authority for steps like this is section 80 of the Companies Act 1985.

[145] Hence the speed and frequency with which US banks such as Citigroup were able to tap sovereign wealth funds for fresh capital in the wake of the sub-prime crisis in 2007. Directors of US companies do have a general duty to look after the interests of their shareholders, who can go to court to argue that they are being disadvantaged by new share issues.

[146] In the UK the 2004 Myners report "The Impact of Shareholders' Pre-emption rights on a Public Company's' Ability to Raise New Capital" looked at the subject in detail, particularly in relation to the capital needs in the biotech sector.

Suggested Reading

Chapter 1 - Defining Corporate Actions

'Corporate Actions Processing, What Are The Risks?' (Oxera, 2004)

Although this report, commissioned by the DTCC of the US, is now a few years old it includes some good statistics for the corporate actions industry and highlights some of the industry's challenges and areas of vulnerability.

Chapter 2 – The Main Corporate Actions

'Share Prices And Trading Activity Over The Corporate Action Processing Cycle' (Oxera, 2006)

Another study commissioned by DTCC, which looks at the impact of takeovers, spin-offs, stock splits, exchange offers and rights issues on share prices and trading volumes. The research was based mainly on a large sample of US corporate actions from 2003 to 2005.

Chapter 4 – The Corporate Actions Industry

'Transforming Corporate Actions Processing' (DTCC, 2003)

This white paper gives a good overview of DTCC's thinking on its role in the corporate actions processing industry at the time.

DTCC's Global Corporate Action validation service

Newsletter, published monthly, which keeps readers abreast of the organisation's work in the corporate action arena. (Available from **www.dtcc.com**)

'Statement On The Need For Universal, Standardised Messaging In Corporate Actions' (Association of Global Custodians, June 2007)

This white paper provides a useful snapshot of the workings of the corporate actions industry (together with a helpful diagram). AGC is an interest group of just 10 global custodians and, apart from its annual survey of securities depositories, this paper is the high point of its output.

Chapter 5 – How Well is The Corporate Actions System Working?

'Managing Risk in Corporate Actions: How Far Has The Industry Come?' (Financial Services Research, April 2006)

A helpful article drawing together the thinking of some of the leading practitioners in the corporate actions field.

'CloseUp – Corporate Actions; Risks? – A quantitative study' (SegaInterSettle)

This is the only honest analysis of the problems facing a Central Securities Depository currently in the public domain.

For an idea of the kinds of problems that corporate actions processing can run into, a look at some of Euroclear UK & Ireland's Corporate Action Bulletins is illuminating and recommended.

Chapter 8 – Shareholder Voting

'Review of The Impediments to Voting UK Shares' (Report by Paul Myners to the Shareholder Voting Working Group, June 2004)

Chapter 10 – Corporate Actions in Different Jurisdictions

'Harmonisation of Corporate Actions Processing in Europe: Giovannini 3' (April 2007)

This report provides a useful list of the areas in which harmonisation was deemed to be necessary and a brief outline of progress in the individual EU-member states.

'China's Capital Markets at The Birth of A New Era' (Araceli Almazan & Kris Huishan Lin, UC Davis School of Law, May 2006)

A useful summary of China's state share reform that takes the form of an interview with Winston W Ma, vice-president at JPMorgan.

Chapter 12 – Corporate Action Effects Across the Investing Spectrum

The DTCC has published the following white papers on the subject of structured securities processing:

'A Central Counterparty for Mortgage-Backed Securities: Paving The Way' (April, 2006)

'Structured Securities Processing Challenges' (June, 2006)

'Transforming Structured Securities Processing' (September, 2007)

Index

Subjects covered in the Glossary are highlighted in bold type.

D

E

eBook edition

As a buyer of the print edition of *Corporate Actions – A Concise Guide*
you can now download the eBook edition free of charge to read on an
eBook reader, your smart phone or your computer.
Simply go to: **http://ebooks.harriman-house.com/corporateactions**
or point your smart phone at the QRC below.

You can then register and download your eBook copy of the book.
www.harriman-house.com

7529438R00128

Printed in Great Britain
by Amazon.co.uk, Ltd.,
Marston Gate.